PRAYING the
PARABLES

A SPIRITUAL
JOURNEY
THROUGH THE
STORIES OF JESUS

Joyce Huggett

InterVarsity Press
Downers Grove, Illinois

Cover photograph: Tony Stone Images/Andy Sacks

ISBN 0-8308-1355-1

Printed in the United States of America ∞

Library of Congress Cataloging-in-Publication Data

Huggett, Joyce, 1937—
    Praying the parables: a spiritual journey through the stories of Jesus/Joyce Huggett.
        p.   cm.
    Includes bibliographical references.
    ISBN 0-8308-1355-1
    1. Sower (Parable)   2. Good Samaritan (Parable)   I. Title.
BT378.S7H84   1997
226.8'06—dc21   97-17076
                                                                         CIP

20   19   18   17   16   15   14   13   12   11   10   9   8   7   6   5   4   3   2   1

13   12   11   10   09   08   07   06   05   04   03   02   01   00   99   98   97

For Ken and Mickey and,
of course, Sara,
with fond memories
and so many thanks

Acknowledgments ———— 9
Introduction: Puzzling over the Parables ———— 11
  Jesus: The New Testament's Number-One Theologian

1. THE PURPOSE & POWER OF THE PARABLE ———— 17
  The Power of a Story
  The Power of the Parable
  The Gulf Between Western and Middle Eastern Learning Styles

2. KEYS THAT UNLOCK THE PARABLES ———— 27
  How to Think Crossculturally
  Identifying the Audience

THE PARABLE OF THE SOWER ———— 37

3. UNDERSTANDING THE PARABLE OF THE SOWER ———— 39
  The Sower
  Rocky Ground
  The Weed Patch and the Harvest
  Processing the Parable
  The Disciples' Reflections
  The Sacrament of Waiting
  The Assurance of Harvest

4. PRAYING THE PARABLE OF THE SOWER ———— 52
  Watching an Action Replay
  Rewriting the Story
  Stepping into the Story
  Some Spiritual Stock-Taking
  Focus on the Person of the Sower

Praying with Mental Pictures
Praying with Images of Failure
Visual Aids

THE PARABLE OF THE GOOD SAMARITAN ————— *71*

5. UNDERSTANDING THE PARABLE OF THE
   GOOD SAMARITAN ————— *73*
   Putting the Parable in Context
   The Priest
   The Levite
   Praying This Part of the Parable

6. THE GOOD SAMARITAN ————— *85*

7. PRAYING THE PARABLE OF THE
   GOOD SAMARITAN ————— *94*
   Preparing to Pray
   Praying the Parable
   Hurting at Gut Level
   Petitionary Prayer
   Living Prayer
   "You Did It for Me . . ."
   Spiritual Stock-Taking
   Letting the Pictures Speak
   The Picture of the Priest Passing By on the Other Side
   Personalizing the Prayer

Epilogue: The Most Memorable Parable
   of Them All ————— *116*
Notes ————— *119*

Acknowledgments

"Very, very many thanks." That's what I want to say to so many people as this book goes to print.

Countless people have prayed the manuscript into being. Some are known to me. Others are anonymous. I send my warmest thanks to you all.

In addition to these friends, acquaintances and prayer supporters, I would like to name four individuals. First, my husband, who read the first draft of the book and, as always, spurred me on with his enthusiastic response and shrewd comments. Next, David Wavre, who, similarly, gave the book a warm and generous reception when I sent it to him. My friend and mentor Pauline Gallagher also deserves an accolade. She gave me hours of her time at the proofreading and revision stages. I was recovering from a prolonged period of illness at this stage of the proceedings. When my energy flagged, Pauline stayed alongside me, prayed, pored over the manuscript herself, cooked some of my meals and generally cheered me on.

Most of all, my heartfelt thanks fly to America to Kenneth Bailey. Ken was also ill when we invited him to comment on the first draft of the manuscript. I therefore imagined that he would simply take a cursory glance at what I had written and make one or two comments. Instead, even when his own energy level was low, he went through the manuscript with a fine-tooth comb and took the trouble to send pages of detailed comments. When I read what he had written, I felt honored and humbled that he should have taken so much time and poured out so much energy on my behalf. As I wove his suggestions into the manuscript, I could see how much readers would benefit from them.

Thank you too to Wendy Ward for her kind permission to reproduce her poem "The Field," featured on pages 58-59.

To all these who believe in this book, I give my profound thanks, praying that its contents may prove as life-changing for others as they have been for me.

PUZZLING OVER THE PARABLES

L*et's do a jigsaw puzzle." That's what my brothers and I* often used to say on cold winter evenings when we were children. We would choose a puzzle, tip all the pieces onto the dining-room table and feverishly start fitting them together. First we fixed the "edgy pieces," as we used to call them, then the easy bits. Finally, and less energetically, we pored over the pile of pieces that all looked alike and that seemed reluctant to become part of the picture. When the puzzle was eventually completed, we would gaze at it with pride, sometimes even fingering it admiringly. Very occasionally, though, we would discover that a piece of the picture was missing. I still remember how devastated I felt on such occasions. A hole in the jigsaw puzzle seemed to bore a hole of disappointment into my heart.

For over forty years, I felt similarly frustrated and let down by the parables of Jesus. I had been conversant with them since childhood, had made an in-depth study of them at college, and had written essays about them that satisfied my tutors. Yet these stories still mystified and confused me.

☐ Why did Jesus tell a string of stories that seem wide open to misinterpretation?

☐ Why didn't he use the more familiar conceptual teaching for which we applaud Paul?

☐ How are these curious similes to be interpreted?

☐ What does the recurring phrase "the kingdom of heaven" mean?

Questions like these plagued me, as did others: Whose explanation of the parables should we accept? The allegorization that used to be fashionable in some theological circles? Or should we reject the insistence that every part of the parable is an allegory? Should we instead accept the hypothesis that each parable contains one main theme?

If we choose the second suggestion and attempt to focus on the one main theme, whose main theme do we accept? Take the parable of the sower, for example: Did Jesus tell this story to persuade his listeners to become fellow harvesters with him? Some theologians maintain that is the main theme of this parable. Or did Jesus tell the story of the sower to underline that the Word of God is rarely readily accepted? Other authorities claim that this is the main theme of the story.

Such claims and counterclaims wearied, confused and frustrated me. Many of the allegories seemed bizarre—like the insistence that for the word *path* we should always read "mind" because the mind is the path along which evil travels. Some of the "main themes" suggested seemed to me to miss the point entirely. Like many other Christians, I learned to live with the glaring gap in the jigsaw puzzle of my understanding of Jesus' teaching and concentrated instead on the teaching of Paul. Until a challenge from a fellow writer sent me scuttling back to the parables.

A group of contributors to Scripture Union's *Alive to God*

Bible-reading notes used to meet from time to time for mutual encouragement, discussion of policies and training. One life-changing day we seemed to spend an inordinate amount of time discussing the Bible's apparent attitude toward women. One member of the group, I noticed, remained unusually quiet while ideas shuttled back and forth. Suddenly, however, he showed that he had not been catnapping. He had been weighing carefully the opinions that had been voiced. Now, he dropped a conversation-stopper into the debate. His argument went something like this: "I notice that this discussion has majored on Paul's teaching. But surely we must always keep Paul's comments in context. Paul didn't precede Jesus. Jesus preceded Paul. Through his teaching, his attitudes and his example, Jesus laid the theological foundations on which Paul later built. Paul's theology must therefore always be placed against the backdrop of his Master's teaching, attitudes and example."

Something stirred inside me as I absorbed the implications of this claim. My reaction had nothing to do with the subject under debate—the Bible's attitude toward women. That was not an issue that raised my hackles in those days. The reaction had more to do with the ring-of-truth quality of my colleague's claim. The awakening of that dormant "something" inside me prompted me to resolve that I would soak myself afresh in the teaching of Jesus—including those riddles, the parables.

I not only returned to a study of the parables, but meditated on them too. Studying the parables still seemed sadly sterile. Meditating on them, however, produced much more fruit. I think of the time when, in my imagination, I slipped into the sandals of the wayward youth in Jesus' parable of the prodigal son (Lk 15). The father's forgiveness humbled me. His embrace consoled me. The lavishness of his felt love convinced me, on a deeper level than ever before, of the truth of Ruth Burrows's claim: "God is obsessed with us, wholly absorbed with caring for us. . . . He has all the passionate, intense concern of the most loving of parents."[1]

I spelled out some of these insights to mission partners attending a Church Mission Society conference on one occasion. After one of the sessions, then-General Secretary Bishop Michael Nazir-Ali asked me a question: "Have you ever come across the writings of Professor Kenneth Bailey?" I confessed that I had never even heard of Ken Bailey, let alone read his books. "I think you'd find his insights illuminating and inspiring," the bishop continued. I determined to track down Bailey's books and eventually bought two bound into one volume: *Poet and Peasant* and *Through Peasant Eyes*. If I claimed that my mind was enlightened, I would be making a gross understatement. I felt like someone whose mind had suddenly been floodlit and whose heart had been strangely touched. I also became increasingly excited by Bailey's claim that Jesus leaves many of his parables unfinished. Take three one-sentence parables that Luke records in quick succession:

> As they were walking along the road, a man said to him, "I will follow you wherever you go." Jesus replied, "Foxes have holes and birds of the air have nests, but the Son of Man has no place to lay his head." He said to another man, "Follow me." But the man replied, "Lord, first let me go and bury my father." Jesus said to him, "Let the dead bury their own dead, but you go and proclaim the kingdom of God." Still another said, "I will follow you, Lord; but first let me go back and say good-by to my family." Jesus replied, "No one who puts his hand to the plow and looks back is fit for service in the kingdom of God." (Lk 9:57-62)

Do these men follow Jesus or not? We are not told. The parables are left suspended—like the ending of an episode of a soap opera. "The reader is obliged to complete the conversation with his own response."[2]

No wonder meditating on the parables seems to bear more fruit than merely studying them, I thought when I registered this claim. I never dreamed, while I was turning such claims over and over in my mind, that I would one day meet the author. In

1992, however, my husband and I spent the entire summer on the island of Cyprus. Among other things, we attended an orientation camp for mission partners in the Troodos mountains. To my amazement and joy, one of the speakers was Kenneth Bailey, who, at that time, was canon theologian of Nicosia Cathedral. He spoke on the parables.

Jesus: The New Testament's Number-One Theologian

I listened, enthralled. At last, I understood why "something had stirred within me" all those years ago. Bailey was giving me a handle to that "something" by giving Jesus a title that startled me at first. He called Jesus a theologian. A very serious theologian. A first-class theologian. "He is *the* theologian of the New Testament," he claimed.

He went on to clarify what he meant. Paul is the kind of theologian Westerners are accustomed to—an abstract theologian who thinks and teaches in concepts. Jesus, on the other hand, is a metaphorical theologian. His parables are not illustrations. Neither are they "the sugar-coating on the theological pill."[3] They are metaphors. In the teaching of Jesus his metaphor is his theology. His parables carry their own weight and message. They penetrate our defenses and are therefore capable of communicating with us on a very deep level if we will let them.

As I listened, the scales fell from my eyes. Suddenly I saw why Jesus taught through stories rather than concepts. Suddenly I understood why the parables lend themselves more to meditation than to study. Suddenly I sensed that most parables do not encapsulate one main theme. Far from it. Embedded in most of Jesus' stories is a web of themes—what Bailey calls "the theological cluster."

Shortly after that orientation camp, the call to my husband and me to come to Cyprus to live seemed to be clarified. Since moving here, we have returned each summer to the Troodos mountains to lead retreats at a very special campsite. On that same campsite, a favorite holiday hideaway for Ken and his wife and daughter, our friendship with the Baileys grew. Ken's books are scholarly. They make demanding reading. "Why don't you write the same way you speak?" I asked him after hearing him preach a powerful sermon in the small church we attend on Troodos. As I got to know him better, I realized that for him to write in the way I was suggesting would cramp his style. "Would you allow to *me* write up some of your insights in a reader-friendly fashion?" I asked one day. His face lit up: "I'd be delighted" was his ready and genuine response.

And so this book was born. Touched and honored by his trust, I read his books, listened to his audiocassettes, watched his videos and prayed with his insights for two years. Inevitably, then, I convey his insights through the filter of my own understanding and prayer and interweave them with my own. I pass them on for several reasons: because they handed me the missing piece of my theological puzzle, because they have provided me with a wealth of material for biblical meditation and prayer, and because, if my own experience is anything to go by, they come packed with the potential for providing people with a way of expressing to God precisely what is on their heart at any given moment. They also contain the potential for discovering how God is prompting them to act in the here and now.

When my colleague's comment first prompted me to return to the parables, my response was dutiful rather than joyful. Duty turned to attraction when I read Ken Bailey's books. Attraction became an ever-deepening friendship as I prayed with the parables. Familiarity turned to commitment when I discovered what a wealth of material for meditation hides in these seemingly simple but profound stories.

Part of that commitment is to pass on to my readers some of the insights that have changed my perception and lifestyle. I do so with the prayer that the lives of others may be as enriched by praying the parables as mine has been.

ONE

THE PURPOSE
& POWER OF THE
PARABLE

W*hy do you speak to people in parables?" That's a question* the disciples put to Jesus after he had told his first story, the parable of the sower.

What a surprising question! These men were Jews. They would have known that Old Testament scholars did their theological thinking in pictures rather than in abstractions. They would have known that prophets and poets alike bring their teaching to a climax with unforgettable stories and images. So instead of writing, "God quiets and comforts believers," the psalmist claims: "I am content and at peace. As a child lies quietly in its mother's arms, so my heart is quiet within me" (Ps 131:2, my paraphrase). As the nineteenth-century Jewish-Christian New Testament scholar Alfred Edersheim asserts, "Jewish writers extol parables because they place the meaning of the law within reach of the comprehension of men."[1]

Were the disciples perplexed by Jesus' stories because he started to tell them suddenly? That's a suggestion one theologian makes. Jesus' early teaching was hard-hitting and forthright, uncompromising and clear:

You're familiar with the command . . . "Do not murder." I'm telling you that anyone who is so much as angry with a brother or sister is guilty of murder. . . .

You know the next commandment pretty well, too: "Don't go to bed with another's spouse." But don't think you've preserved your virtue simply by staying out of bed. Your *heart* can be corrupted by lust even quicker than your *body*. Those leering looks you think nobody notices—they also corrupt. . . .

You're familiar with the old written law, "Love your friend," and its unwritten companion, "Hate your enemy." I'm challenging that. I'm telling you to love your enemies. Let them bring out the best in you, not the worst. . . .

In a word, what I'm saying is, *Grow up*. You're kingdom subjects. Now live like it. Live out your God-created identity. Live generously and graciously toward others, the way God lives toward you.[2]

If such dynamic teaching sent a shiver of excitement down the disciples' spines, their bewildered reaction to the seemingly tame, enigmatic story of the sower is, perhaps, understandable.

Edersheim suggests another reason why Jesus changed style midstream. Over a period of time, Jesus' audience arranged themselves into two parties. On the one hand, his teaching was attracting huge crowds and being received with enthusiasm. Countless people were becoming disciples (some permanently, some for a short while only). On the other hand, the Pharisees' opposition party, which insisted that Jesus' teaching was Satanic, was gaining momentum also. Into this ferment Jesus dropped a series of pithy, punchy, mind-bending stories. He explains why: "To create readiness, to nudge the people toward

receptive insight" (Mt 13:13).[3] As he put it to his disciples:
You've been given insight into God's kingdom. You know
how it works. Not everybody has this gift, this insight; it
hasn't been given to them. Whenever someone has a ready
heart for this, the insights and understandings flow freely.
But if there is no readiness, any trace of receptivity soon
disappears. That's why I tell stories: to create readiness, to
nudge the people toward receptive insight. In their present
state they can stare till doomsday and not see it, listen till
they're blue in the face and not get it. . . . But you have
God-blessed eyes—eyes that see! And God-blessed ears—
ears that hear![4]

There it is in a nutshell. The purpose of the parables is not
simply to entertain or to inform the mind. No. The main
purpose of the parables is to evoke from the listeners a God-
blessed—that is, a Holy Spirit-inspired—openness. A response
of the heart.

The Power of a Story

The Old Testament reveals how a simple story can achieve this
aim. For example, that poignant story the prophet Nathan told
to King David after he had seduced a subject's wife. The
Israelite army was at war, but David had not gone to battle with
the troops. He had remained at home. Walking around the flat
roof of his palace one evening, he looked down on the garden
of Uriah, one of his commanders. There he feasted on the
alluring form of Uriah's wife, Bathsheba. Consumed with lust
for her, he had her brought to his palace, where he committed
adultery with her. Subsequently, as a result of the king's scheming, Uriah was killed in action, and Bathsheba became David's
wife.

I often wonder how pastors in the West today might disci-
pline a member of their congregation convicted of such a crime.
Some would doubtless withhold Communion from the culprit.

Others would demand a public confession. Still others would excommunicate the criminal. All would be aiming to achieve the same goal: to help the individual face up to the magnitude and implications of his actions.

God, on the other hand, acts quite differently. In the words of Samuel: "The LORD sent Nathan to David" (2 Sam 12:1) to ask the king the reason he had despised God's word by doing what was evil in his eyes (v. 9). God gave Nathan the unenviable task of confronting David with his adulterous, murderous behavior.

In true Middle Eastern fashion, Nathan goes to the king and tells a tearjerker of a story. We would do well to read it slowly, trying to picture the prophet spinning this yarn for his king. We would do well, too, to picture the scene Nathan describes. We might even attempt to enter into Nathan's story ourselves and register the emotions that surface in us as we do so:

> There were two men in a certain town, one rich and the other poor. The rich man had a very large number of sheep and cattle, but the poor man had nothing except one little ewe lamb he had bought. He raised it, and it grew up with him and his children. It shared his food, drank from his cup and even slept in his arms. It was like a daughter to him.
>
> Now a traveler came to the rich man, but the rich man refrained from taking one of his own sheep or cattle to prepare a meal for [him]. . . . Instead, he took the ewe lamb that belonged to the poor man and prepared it for the one who had come to him. (2 Sam 12:1-4)

The story incensed David. Believing that Nathan was relating an incident that had happened in his own kingdom, he "burned with anger against the man" (v. 5). His sense of right and wrong had been quickened. He demanded justice: "The man who did this deserves to die! He must pay for that lamb four times over, because he did such a thing and had no pity" (v. 6).

Nathan's work is nearly done. He has no need to convince

David of the despicable, deceitful, sinful nature of the crime. The story has done that for him. David's response proves it. Nathan now needs only to expose David's culpability. He does so with one slash of the tongue: "You are the man!" (v. 7). How these words must have stung. This is the power of the story.

Stories speak as powerfully to the uneducated as to the educated. A group of illiterate tribal women in Pakistan taught me this on one occasion. I was squatting with them on the mud floor of a room in a Bible college. Their husbands were sitting on chairs around and behind us. We were listening to my husband expound Ephesians 5:25: "Husbands, love your wives, just as Christ loved the church and gave himself up for her." I watched the women while my husband told story after story of men who had cherished their wives and poured on them the kind of tender, liberating, unconditional, forgiving love with which Jesus loves his church. Incredulity filled the women's eyes. Smiles of hope spread across their faces. Heads nodded with delight as, gradually, they grasped some of the implications of this verse. Some even stifled giggles of joy as they heard my husband insist that their husbands were to love them with the superlative love with which Jesus loves us.

These women wouldn't have been capable of following an erudite sermon. They were delightfully capable of entering into theology Jesus-style: theology distilled in simple but profound stories. In fact, they listened to it with rapt attention.

The Power of the Parable

Stories speak to more than our minds; they appeal to and stir our emotions. As contemporary author Sallie Te Selle puts it: "We are bodies that think, not minds that think." In other words, we do not think like computers or robots; vibrant emotions pulsate just below the surface of our thought processes even though we do not always heed these feelings.

Parables are often stories—stories that place one thing alongside another. In Hebrew and Arabic, the word *parable* also embraces a whole variety of figurative speech: allegories, fables, proverbs, apocalyptic revelations, riddles, symbols, pseudo-nyms and fictitious people. The Old Testament is full of such picture language. My training as a teacher of the deaf helps me to understand why. People with limited language need pictures. The visual bypasses words yet illuminates the mind.

In our relationship with an infinite, omnipotent, holy God, we are people with limited language. We therefore need pic-tures and symbols, stories and other visual stimuli to help us comprehend the incomprehensible. God gives such pictures:

"My thoughts are not your thoughts,
    neither are your ways my ways,"
        declares the LORD.

"As the heavens are higher than the earth,
    so are my ways higher than your ways
    and my thoughts than your thoughts." (Is 55:8-9)

No carefully culled sermon can do justice to the picture. Words might clarify the concepts in which the picture is encased: My thoughts are not your thoughts, my ways are not your ways, my ways are higher than your ways, my thoughts are higher than your thoughts. But words would dilute God's passionate proclamation: "As the heavens are higher than the earth . . ."

Invite a congregation to venture outdoors, however; invite them to stand and gaze in turn at the sky, the earth and the immense gulf that separates them—then they will understand because they will see. Seeing, they will engage with the imagery. That at least is what has happened for groups with whom I have contemplated the night sky. As we've gazed from the star-stud-ded heavens to the shadowy earth and back again, we've found ourselves strangely awestruck. As we've tried to measure the unfathomable distance between the full moon and the rolling fields onto which it pours its eerie light, we've found ourselves dumbstruck. There are no words to describe such beauty, such majesty, such awe, such vastness, such otherness, such grandeur. The mystery of God defies definition or interpretation.

Or take that familiar passage, Isaiah 53:7: "He was oppressed and afflicted, yet he did not open his mouth; he was led like a lamb to the slaughter, and as a sheep before her shearers is silent, so he did not open his mouth." Again, no three-point sermon can hope to interpret this picture adequately. The picture itself speaks more powerfully than any words.

I once watched a shepherd shearing a sheep before taking it to the slaughterhouse. The image of that silent, struggling, suffering creature rises before my eyes every time I read Isaiah's prophecy or sing that well-loved reflection on it: "Led like a lamb to the slaughter . . ." The picture possesses a power no words possess. As Ken Bailey rightly reminds us, "For centuries, thoughtful contemplation on this parable of the lamb before its killer and shearer has taken readers into depths of meaning no interpretation could afford."[5] That is why he stresses the need to delve into the details of the story itself—to let the metaphor do its own work. "It is the play of the images that does the job."[6]

The reason we need to delve into the story and contemplate the picture is that a parable has one single purpose: not to inform the mind but to *elicit a response of the heart.*

The Gulf Between Western and Middle Eastern Learning Styles

Jesus, we must remember, was not a Western theologian. He was a Middle Eastern theologian. Undoubtedly, that is the chief reason he used stories and similes to elicit a response from his listeners.

The dominant Western way of teaching differs dramatically from the Middle Eastern method. Since the fifth century B.C.

and the rise of classical Greece, Western teachers have created meaning mainly with concepts that they may illustrate with metaphors or similes; Middle Eastern teachers, on the other hand, have created meaning mainly with similes, metaphors, parables and dramatic action (all four of which the Old Testament calls parables, as we have seen).

When a Westerner wants to process thoughts, he or she chooses words and concepts carefully. These words and concepts are processed primarily with the intellect. A teacher or a preacher might occasionally illustrate his or her ideas with a story or a simile or a metaphor—but the illustration is peripheral. The concept is the vital ingredient, so much so that if the audience or congregation is considered intelligent and alert, the speaker might dispense with illustrations altogether. He or she might even fear that the listeners would feel insulted by such window dressing. If readers or listeners are capable of grasping concepts, why waste time serving them picture language?

I was amused to catch myself adopting this philosophy while typing this chapter. In the outline I had scribbled: "Illustrate here." By this I meant "give an illustration at this point in the manuscript." As I was writing the above paragraph, however, I became aware of the conversation I was having with myself: *Surely there's no need to give an illustration. Readers are intelligent people. They'll find an example intrusive, unnecessary. Anyway, it'll take up a lot of space.*

If I had been writing mainly for Middle Easterners, however, I would not have chatted to myself in this way. Instead of starting with a concept and illustrating it, I would have started with a simile or a story, a metaphor or a picture. I have discovered that this is the way to capture Middle Easterners' attention and to teach them theology.

I learned this while leading a retreat for a group of Cypriots shortly after I moved to the island. I quickly discerned that the attention span of this group seemed short while they were being fed with concepts. So instead of giving them the talk I had prepared on Jesus' parable of the vine and the branches, I changed my plan. The place where we were holding the retreat was surrounded by vineyards. *These people have been brought up in a culture that has cultivated grapes for centuries,* I reasoned to myself. *Their lives have been steeped in the symbolism Jesus uses. They will probably glean more from gazing and meditating on the vines than from a talk given by me.* I made a suggestion aloud: "I'd like you to take your Bibles and notebooks outside and find a place in the vineyard where you can sit quietly by yourself to read John 15:1-8. Gaze at the vine and the branches and let Jesus speak to you."

The mood of the group changed immediately. With obvious anticipation they set off for the vineyard. When they returned, their thoughts bubbled out of them. A former vine-dresser set the ball rolling. "I read Jesus' words about pruning," he said, "and I remembered how we used to cut back not just the dead branches but the fruitful branches as well. The pruning was for greater quality and greater quantity." He continued, "I realized that parts of my life need pruning. My prayer asks God to cut away what shouldn't be there."

Others said that they had stared and stared at the seemingly disfigured stump of the vine. Their gazing turned to wonder as they observed how the stump had given birth to so many sturdy branches that had spread so far. The realization dawned, though, that if those branches were ever severed from the stump, they would become useless. Their contemplation triggered a prayer: that they might make their home in God—always.

The sharing thrilled me. My carefully prepared Western-style talk on the vine had not been needed. It would have failed utterly to elicit the heart-responses that were expressed. God's handiwork, his visual parable, had succeeded where I would have only failed.

My new Cypriot friends were receiving spiritual insights not merely into their minds but also into their hearts. I use *heart* deliberately and in the biblical sense of the word: meaning the mind *and* the emotions, the intellect *and* the senses, the imagination *and* the will. They had convinced me of the truth of T. W. Manson's claim: "The true parable is not an illustration to help one through a theological discussion; it is rather *a mode of religious experience.* . . . It is not a crutch for limping intellects, but *a spurt to religious insight:* its object is not to provide simple theological instruction, but *to produce living religious faith.* . . . Every true parable is a call to a better life and a deeper trust in God."[7]

My friends had embodied for me Ken Bailey's insistence that in metaphorical theology the metaphor does not illustrate a fine theological point. The metaphor *is* the theology. They had raised a question for me: What changes lives rather than simply stretches minds? Is it the customary Western way of processing data, or rather the Middle Eastern approach of opening "the heart," the whole self, to the truth?

TWO

KEYS THAT UNLOCK THE PARABLES

T*he New Testament's number-one theologian is Jesus.*
Jesus did not tell stories to illustrate his theology. His stories
are his theology. The reason Jesus chose to present his teaching
in this way was that he wanted to elicit a heart-response from
his listeners. In this chapter we'll examine the importance of
placing the parables in their historical and cultural context.
We'll also explore ways in which we might best be able to cross
centuries and eras so that we can place ourselves in Palestine as
it was in the first century.

The main reason we will explore these subjects is that the
Word of God was spoken through people at given moments in
time and in a particular culture. It follows that when applying
our minds to the parables, we need to stand, as it were, at the
back of the audience to whom Jesus first told the story and,
while standing on tiptoe, to listen as intently as we can to what

he is saying. When we see the pictures Jesus paints through the eyes and perception of the people he originally addressed, when we hear his stories through their language, their culture, their history, when we tune into their sensitivities and their value systems, we become receptive both to the original message—what Jesus said to his listeners—and to today's message—what he is saying to us.

We also notice that Jesus addresses sinners in need of grace. We therefore qualify. The story is as significant for us as it was for the original audience. In turn, the story is able to penetrate our spirit on the deepest level. In other words, the history, the culture and the value systems are three of the keys to a comprehensive unlocking of the parable.

The more I live crossculturally, the more I am convinced of the importance of this principle. As communication experts remind us, even the most lucid message depends not only on the speaker, but on the listener also. The diagram below demonstrates this.

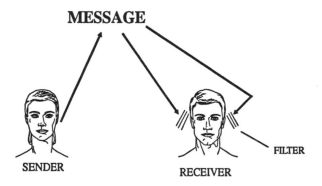

When words leave a speaker's lips, they are picked up by a listener's ears, filtered through the listener's perception, emotions, attitudes, experience, relationships and value systems, and interpreted accordingly. Say the word *father* to a group of children, for example, and you may well receive a mixed reaction. Some of the children may have a father they rarely see.

Others may have a father who abuses or beats them, and still others may have a tender, kind, patient, generous father. Each child will interpret the familiar word *father* in the light of their experience.

If a common word like *father* can cause confusion, how much more misunderstanding can be created by trying to import Middle Eastern concepts into other cultures that each have their own value system. Inform a person from China, for example, that the Promised Land overflows with milk and honey, and the listener will almost certainly be filled not with anticipation but with disgust. In China dairy products are not prized and valued; they are considered unclean and inedible.

The differing perceptions and value systems that separated me from the illiterate Pakistani tribal women I mentioned in chapter one concerned me deeply. That was the reason, as I listened to my husband expound Paul's injunction "Husbands, love your wives, just as Christ loved the church," I asked myself: *What are these women hearing him say?* After all, these women are not allowed to go out of the home alone. They must always cover their heads when in the presence of men. They have been brought up to believe that they are inferior to men. Their life revolves around their husband, their children, the home, the extended family, the tribe. Phenomena like education and travel do not concern them. Until they met me, they had never encountered anyone who did not speak their language. Consequently, they believed that the whole world speaks Urdu. How, then, do we begin to communicate the gospel to such people in a way they can truly grasp?

With the differences that divided us in the front of my mind, I wondered how I would feel if the situation were reversed—if I were listening to a Pakistani preach the same sermon in Urdu with an interpreter translating it to me in English. That prompted another train of thought: Suppose Jesus had been a Pakistani coming from one of these remote tribal villages.

Suppose his parables were then translated into English. I would expect that in certain places the text would seem strange, incomprehensible. I would anticipate that from time to time I would be incapable of picking up the innuendos and insinuations because I have only a limited understanding of the culture. I would expect that if I could hear him tell his stories to Pakistanis, there would be times when the audience might be deeply shocked and I would not understand the reason because of my lack of familiarity with cultural norms and taboos. I would also expect that there would be times when the audience would laugh, leaving me in the dark because I don't know the culture's jokes. I would expect to find myself missing out on a profound layer of perception unless, somehow, I could project myself into the culture of the hillsides and familiarize myself with the lifestyle and mindset of tribal village people.

Jesus was not a Pakistani from a remote tribal village. He was a first-century Palestinian living in the hillside village of Nazareth. The cultural gap between the West and his culture is as marked as the gulf that sadly separated me from these women.

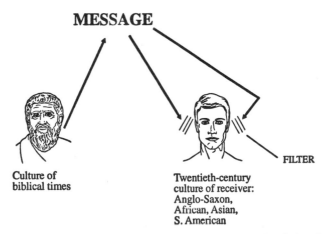

MESSAGE

Culture of
biblical times

Twentieth-century
culture of receiver:
Anglo-Saxon,
African, Asian,
S. American

FILTER

There is another reason it is important to step back in time to the first century and over in space to Palestine. If we fail to do this, we may well find ourselves substituting our own culture for the Middle Eastern culture that was the setting for Jesus' theology.

One renowned authority on the parables did just this on one occasion. Commenting on the story of the prodigal son, he notes that the father, having embraced his returning son, turns around to address his servants. This must mean, he surmises, that father and son had by this time returned to the house. No servant, he asserts, would run out of the house and down the road.

As Ken Bailey points out, this theologian was clearly reading the parable through thoroughly Western spectacles. When he read the word *servant*, he seems to have had in his mind's eye a stiff and starchy nineteenth-century British butler whose dignity would be severely dented if he ran down a British street. That, of course, is a far cry from the picture Jesus intended us to see when he told the story. Anyone who has lived in the Middle East would know that. Anyone familiar with the Middle East would know that any drama attracts a crowd. In Middle Eastern villages even today, everything is public. Middle Easterners are gregarious. There is a total absence of English reserve or Western sophistication.

In Cyprus, for example, when a couple gets married, it is not a private family affair. It is a public celebration. Guests, including strangers, flock to the party. They are genuinely welcomed, with or without an invitation. They join in the feasting and the chatting and the dancing.

A Westerner would not know that unless he or she had experienced hospitality in this part of the world. It underlines the need we have to soak ourselves, as much as we are able, in the culture of the time when Jesus told his tales and in the culture of the place where he told them.

How to Think Crossculturally

A challenge like that raises a pressing question: How do we step back in time and over in space so that we can project ourselves into Palestine as Jesus knew it? Ken Bailey discovered a way. That is one reason why his books, videos and sermons have brought the parables to life for hundreds of his readers, students and friends. Ken was fortunate. From an early age he found himself plunged into the kind of culture that would have been familiar to Jesus. The son of missionary parents who spent much of their life working among Middle Eastern peasants, Ken learned Arabic as a child and speaks the language fluently. He also speaks and reads Greek, Syrian, Syriac and Aramaic (the language spoken in the Eastern Mediterranean in Jesus' day).

Familiarity with these languages gives him the respect of peasant people living in remote villages. It also gives him access to ancient versions of the Bible. Over the years he has collected on microfilm and in print more than thirty early Arabic and Syriac versions of and commentaries on the New Testament. These texts come from Israel/Palestine, Egypt, Lebanon, Syria and Iraq, and stretch from the second to the fourteenth centuries. From them he has unearthed rich treasures: perceptions of the Scriptures that grow out of ancient traditional Middle Eastern culture. These insights come to us from centuries of Middle Eastern Christians who themselves are inheritors of the broader Middle Eastern culture of which Jesus was a part.

Ken had not only language to his credit, but an acquaintance with Middle Eastern culture as well. He is a Presbyterian pastor—a warm, outgoing, pied-piper kind of person who attracts a following wherever he goes. For five years he worked in the Middle East with a carefully chosen literacy team. This is how he describes the experience:

I was privileged to live in [Middle Eastern] villages for long periods of time. Naturally, the villages themselves were among the most isolated and primitive, because they were the villages where the highest rates of illiteracy were to be found. Living in the village, I was able to become a part of the scenery and could interact with the village people not as a guest or stranger, researcher or scholar, but as an ordinary resident. With no camera or notebook, I could watch people interacting with each other. Over a period of years, I gradually came to the realization that a new layer of perception is available when we ask a fresh set of questions of the biblical text—questions that revolve around attitudes, relationships, responses, and value judgements.

☐ In this culture, what is the attitude of a sleeping neighbour to a call for help in the night?

☐ In this village, what is the nature of the relationship between a landowner and his tenants?

☐ Supposing a son should ask his father for his inheritance, what kind of response would a father in this culture make?

☐ When a steward reduces the rent, how do the tenants feel about him? What value judgements do they make?[1]

In addition to rooting himself in the culture and conversing with villagers in their own language, Ken preached and administered the sacraments to village congregations across Egypt and Lebanon, Syria and Israel/Palestine. Gradually, intimacy and trust developed between pastor and people. As relationships deepened, Ken was able to probe further. For example, he has what he calls an ongoing "love affair" with the parable of the prodigal son. For over thirty-five years he tried to tease out the implications of the youngest son's request with people from all walks of life from Morocco to India and from Turkey to the Sudan:

"Has anyone in your village ever made such a request?" he would ask. The reply was always the same: "Never!" "Could anyone ever make such a request?" "Impossible!" "If anyone ever did, what would happen?" "His father would beat him, of course!" "Why?" "This request means—he wants his father to die!"[2]

Gradually, conversations like this caused him to draw this conclusion: "I have been privileged to observe what the parables mean when seen through peasant eyes."[3]

One way we can cross the historical and cultural thresholds presented to us by the parables, then, is to learn from the insights that Ken Bailey and others like him spread before us, asking questions rather than making assumptions, questions like the ones that have already been mentioned: How did a first-century Palestinian react when his neighbor knocked on his door in the middle of the night? Was the reaction the same as it would be in the West or the Far East today, or was it different?

Identifying the Audience

One additional question is: Who was Jesus speaking to when he told this parable? In Matthew 13:10, for example, we hear Jesus interpreting the parable of the sower just for his disciples. In Luke 10, however, he tells the story of the good Samaritan for a lawyer who was testing him (v. 25). The parables in Luke 15 are told to a hostile crowd of complaining teachers of the law, while the parable of the vine and the branches in John 15 appears again to have been reserved for his disciples only.

In addition to identifying the audience, there is great value, as we have already noted, in standing at the back of the crowd that was listening to Jesus tell the story and asking: "What did the metaphors he is using communicate to these people?" "What are they hearing him say?" Only then can we understand what he is saying to us.

As we listen and attempt to discern the answers to these questions, it can be helpful to have three more at the back of our mind:

1. *What picture language is Jesus using to hook his listeners?* "A man was going down from Jerusalem to Jericho, when he fell into the hands of robbers." (Lk 10:30). "A farmer went out to sow his seed . . ." (Mt 13:3).

2. *What ultimate response is Jesus pressing his audience to make?* The Pharisee hearing the parable of the prodigal son is

pressed to be reconciled to his "family."[4] The people listening to the story of the sower are pressed to create a home where kingdom seeds can bear fruit.

3. *How does Jesus move from a to b? How does he woo his listeners into a receptive frame of mind?* He "scratches where they itch," as the saying goes. Knowing that they are consumed with longing for the coming of the kingdom, he tells a story that addresses this longing. "The kingdom is here," he claims in the story of the sower. Knowing that the farmers and fishermen in his audience display their emotions readily, he appeals to their feelings. He is well aware that his references to infertile parts of the farmer's field will cause the crowd to identify with the hopes and disappointments of the sower who works for one thing—a bountiful harvest.

In the next section of this book we will observe how these questions help us to keep the parables in their cultural and historical context. We will see too how they enable us to unlock a particular parable for ourselves: how we can pray with it and respond to it.

THE PARABLE
OF THE SOWER

That same day Jesus went out of the house
and sat by the lake. Such large crowds gathered around him that
he got into a boat and sat in it, while all the people
stood on the shore. Then he told them many things in parables,
saying: "A farmer went out to sow his seed.
As he was scattering the seed, some fell along the path,
and the birds came and ate it up. Some fell on rocky places, where it
did not have much soil. It sprang up quickly,
because the soil was shallow. But when the sun came up,
the plants were scorched, and they withered because they had no
root. Other seed fell among thorns,
which grew up and choked the plants. Still other seed fell
on good soil, where it produced a crop—a hundred,
sixty or thirty times what was sown.
He who has ears, let him hear."

MATTHEW 13:1-9

THREE

UNDERSTANDING THE PARABLE OF THE SOWER

Ifwe are to understand the parables of Jesus, we must seek to
project ourselves back in time to first-century Palestine. We
must also seek to stand, as it were, at the back of the particular
audience to whom Jesus originally told the story and let the
details filter through their eyes, their ears, their experience, their
emotions and their mindset to us. Keeping a series of questions
in our minds as we read and meditate on the parables can also
help us to achieve our aim:

□ Who are the people to whom Jesus first tells this story?

□ What hidden agendas do they harbor in their hearts?

□ What do they see in their mind's eye as Jesus' story unfolds?

□ How might they feel as they listen?

□ What is Jesus pressing them to see and sense and hear?

□ What response is he begging them to make?

□ What do they actually hear him say?

In this chapter we will attempt to stand at the back of the crowd that first heard Jesus tell the story of the sower. We will also attempt to listen to the story as though for the first time.

Picture the scene: Jesus is sitting at the water's edge by the Sea of Galilee. Hordes of people are descending on him from all directions—like football fans heading for the game. So many people finally congregate on that particular patch of shore that Jesus is compelled to withdraw to a nearby boat. He proceeds to use this fishing boat as a pulpit.

The Twelve are there (Lk 8:1), that group of men who now live in community with Jesus and are learning what it means to follow him. Certain women are also there (Lk 8:2): Mary Magdalene, Joanna, who is the wife of the manager of Herod's household, Susanna and other women who have already become Jesus' supporters. Like the Twelve, these women are thoroughly committed to this new, charismatic rabbi. Some have already been on the receiving end of his healing ministry. Others have been set free by his deliverance ministry. They seem to be drawn to him as by a magnet. Wherever he goes, they follow.

John the Baptist's devotees are almost certainly there. Jesus' theme on this Galilean tour is the kingdom of God. John's followers have already been exposed to this subject. They've heard John shout more than once, "God's kingdom is here" (Mt 3:2 The Message). They've witnessed the Baptist emerge from the desert looking so much like the promised Elijah that they've flocked to hear him preach. Now John is in prison. Before his imprisonment, however, John pointed to Jesus, claiming that he is the one who will "ignite the kingdom life within you, . . . the Holy Spirit, changing you from the inside out" (Mt 3:11 The Message). Doubtless, then, they're now curious to hear this new prophet.

Representatives of the leading political and religious parties are almost certainly there too. These groups also feel passionate about the coming of the kingdom, but their views on the way the kingdom will be ushered in clash. One party believes that the kingdom of God will be heralded by terrible but necessary tribulation, even violence. Another group insists that the kingdom will be announced by dramatic, supernatural events: the sky will fall and the moon will turn to blood, graves will give up their dead and the earth will open up and swallow the wicked. After these cataclysmic events, the advent of the kingdom will be apparent to all. Still others anticipate a political and military revolt that will, they hope, overthrow Roman rule.

In other words, the audience consists of at least four types of people: the committed (the Twelve), the caring (the women), the curious (John's disciples) and the critical (the religious leaders).

One thing unites these groups: they all eagerly wait and watch for the coming of the kingdom. No prophet has spoken for four hundred years. Yet they remain convinced that they are God's chosen people. Chosen but crushed. Through their dogmatism and fastidiousness the Pharisees are reducing religion to a set of rules and regulations. God is being presented as someone totally "other" to be revered and feared, obeyed and served, but never loved. The richness of relationship with a heavenly Father is neither taught nor modeled. Religion is not presented as the renewal of the soul. Religious observance consists of a series of dos and don'ts that affect family relationships, tithes, food laws, purity laws and, of course, sabbath observance. Rules range from a burdensome form of honoring father and mother to a scrupulous cleansing before preparing or eating meals to a nit-picking set of restrictive laws about what was and was not permissible on the sabbath.

For many spontaneity has been stifled. Countless people have a false, damaging image of God. He is the judge who is to be feared, the demanding one, the tyrant, the punitive policeman who watches over every action and is ready to pounce when his subjects put a foot wrong.

Into this seething sea of popular opinion, Jesus casts a simple story, a story about a sower.

The Sower

The crowd behind which we are standing is conversant with the farming methods of their time. They are part of an agrarian society. When Jesus starts his story with "A farmer went out to sow his seed," they picture the man. They see him striding over his land clutching a bag or a basket of seeds. They know that he will spread the seeds liberally.

A story not only appeals to the mind, it tugs at the emotions as well, especially when the audience consists of people like these who have no inhibitions about betraying their feelings in public.

"Some [seed] fell along the path," Jesus continues. Some of his listeners groan aloud. They know what this means. They know what we may have forgotten or never known—that first-century Palestinian farmers possess not whole fertile fields, but strips of terraced land that are partitioned off by stone walls. Access is gained to a succession of these strips of land by means of a narrow, unplowed, hard-packed, protected public right-of-way: the path. No farmer throws seeds *on* the path. This farmer sows seed *along* the path. The soil along or adjacent to the path is inhospitable. Farmers try to cultivate it, but it's impossible. This is where they back and turn the oxen that pull the cumbersome plow. There is no way the ground here can be plowed or harrowed. Even so, the farmer in Jesus' story takes the risk of sowing precious seed right there.

Rocky Ground

"Some [seed] fell on rocky places, where it did not have much soil," Jesus persists (Mt 13:5). The crowd can imagine it. They know what we may not be aware of—that these terraces now being cultivated were cut like shelves by them or their ancestors out of the steep, rocky hillside.

Are the minds of the crowd taking a trip down memory lane? Are they visualizing those pioneers leveling such soil as there was on this uneven shelf of mountainous rock? Are they watching them descend into the valley with their donkeys to collect more soil? Do they recall what happened—how these early farmers gradually built up their terraces and leveled the soil, how the leveling was still sometimes uneven? Do they see, in their mind's eye, what happens to these terraces when the spring rains fall? Where the soil is shallow, water collects and saturates the earth. Because the soil lacks depth, the earth stays wet. The seeds planted there sprout quickly but die equally quickly. Their roots can no more penetrate the underlying mountain of rock than seeds planted in a seed tray can penetrate hard plastic.

The crowd is not making the mistake succeeding generations of foreigners will make. They are not seeing in their mind's eye an expansive fertile field in which lie a few stones that a lazy farmer has not removed. They know Jesus is describing a field that is solid rock with a layer of soil on top that is too thin in places to sustain agriculture. They know that is the reason the infant seedlings struggle and succumb to the scorching sun.

The Weed Patch and the Harvest

"Other seed fell among thorns, which grew up and choked the plants." Jesus' voice breaks into their reverie. The crowd pictures the scene: tiny seeds tumbling into a virtual forest of waist-high thorns and thistles and sturdy, shoulder-high grasses with matted root masses. Is the crowd cheering the farmer's persistence? Are they applauding his desire that a bountiful harvest should be reaped, come what may? Do they cheer and clap when Jesus brings his story to a crescendo? "Some fell on good earth, and produced a harvest beyond his wildest dreams"

(Mt 13:8 The Message). Or, by now, have their own hidden agendas silenced them? How are they reacting as Jesus gives his challenging conclusion: "Are you listening to this? Really listening?" (Mt 13:9 The Message)?

Jesus' story is finished. Or has it just begun? He has presented us with raw, but live, material. Now he stops talking. He has appealed to our emotions. Now he leaves us to process them. He has made his longing plain. Now he leaves us to respond in our own way and in our own time.

Processing the Parable
The crowd disperses, but they won't forget the story. This is the Middle East. Everything of import in the Middle East is debated. The women will gossip about the story in their gardens, at the well or in the bazaar. The men will debate the story in their meeting places—the equivalent of today's Middle Eastern all-male "coffee shops." The religious leaders will debate the implications of the story in such places as the Sanhedrin, the highest Jewish court during Roman times.

The disciples are fortunate. They can debate the story with Jesus. As we noted in chapter one, they asked him a question: "Why do you tell stories?" "To create readiness," he replies. And adds:

To nudge the people toward receptive insight. . . . In their present state they can stare till doomsday and not see it, listen till they're blue in the face and not get it. I don't want Isaiah's forecast repeated all over again:

"Your ears are open but you don't hear a thing.
     Your eyes are awake but you don't see a thing.
The people are blockheads!
They stick their fingers in their ears
     so they won't have to listen;
They screw their eyes shut
     so they won't have to look,

so they won't have to deal with me face-to-face
and let me heal them. (Mt 13:13 The Message)
"Listen then to what the parable of the sower means," he
continues. "When anyone hears the message about the kingdom . . ." (Mt 13:18). "The message about the kingdom"? Yes.
As he has told them before, the kingdom has arrived. His
kingdom, however, bears no resemblance to the apocalyptic or
political revolutionary disruption anticipated by the religious
leaders of the day. His kingdom is the place where a seed is
quietly planted in the soil of people's hearts.

Jesus is now speaking only to his disciples. These are the
sowers of the future. We now stand at the back of this small
band of men and listen to Jesus' interpretation of his own tale.
Sowing kingdom seeds is a tough, sometimes discouraging task,
Jesus seems to be at pains to warn them. All kinds of hidden
obstacles trap the seeds before they ever have a chance of fusing
with the soil of a person's heart. Take the problem of unprepared hearts and minds, for example. The hearer fails to understand and therefore rejects the seed. Satan then pounces and
snatches the Word before it can take root.

Or what about the common problem of shallowness, emo-
tionalism and lack of stickability? The soil of some people's
hearts is as lacking in depth as the topsoil pioneer farmers spread
on some sections of that terrace where the sower in the story
cast his seed. Because they do not have enough depth to sustain
the growth of the Word of God, the good news receives only a
temporary welcome. When rumblings of trouble or persecution
are heard or when the need to swim against the cultural tide
arises, the rooting of the new growth is blocked. The new plant
shrivels and dies.

Then there's that perennial weed problem. Other people also
accept the seed with eagerness at first. Seedlings that sprout,
though, quickly find themselves vying with "weeds of worry
and illusions about getting more and wanting everything under

the sun" (Mt 13:22 The Message). They are quickly choked and strangled.

What is needed, Jesus insists, is openness of heart and mind. Receptivity. Just as the seed does not force itself on the soil, so the kingdom never forces itself on the listener. It germinates and grows only where it is welcomed—into hearts that are like soft, clean, deep soil.

Sowers must therefore hold two things in tension. Like the sower in the story, they must broadcast kingdom seeds—liberally and generously in every nook and cranny of God's great field, even in seemingly barren, potentially unfruitful places. They must also expect a mixture of success and failure.

But there will be a harvest. Just as much of the farmer's terrace was fertile, so many hearts are open and ready to receive and respond to the news of the kingdom. These will not only hear, but will also produce much fruit, some as much as a hundred times more than was sown.

The Disciples' Reflections

As the disciples reflect on Jesus' story and its interpretation, what do they hear him say? Have they really registered the inevitability of failure? Jesus seems to insist on underlining this theme. On an earlier occasion he warned them that success is not automatic.

I have in my mind those careful instructions Jesus gave his disciples when he trained them for their first mission: "If anyone will not welcome you or listen to your words, shake the dust off your feet when you leave that home or town" (Mt 10:14).

He will express this again using strong language when he sends out the seventy-two: "When you enter a town and are welcomed, eat what is set before you. Heal the sick who are there and tell them, 'The kingdom of God is near you.' But when you enter a town and are not welcomed, go into its streets and say, 'Even the dust of your town that sticks to our feet we wipe off against you' " (Lk 10:8-11).

Did the Twelve realize the clear implications of these instructions? When they sow seeds that fall on unprepared, shallow or weed-ridden soil, the fault lies not with the seed nor with the sower, but rather with the lack of receptivity of the soil. The essential ingredient without which germination, growth and fruit-bearing cannot take place is soft, clean, deep, receptive soil.

Will the Twelve recall this teaching after Jesus' ascension when Paul and Barnabas exercise "the sacrament of the dusting off of the feet"?[1] In Acts 13, we find Paul and Barnabas quite literally shaking the dust from their feet. They had poured themselves into the task of scattering kingdom seeds in Antioch. Countless seeds had evidently begun to fuse with the soil of converts' hearts (v. 48). Some of the leading Jews, however, "seeing the crowds, went wild with jealousy" and, believing their comfortable way of life was on the brink of being destroyed, incited others to persecute the disciples and expel them from the region (v. 50). So Paul and Barnabas shook the dust from their feet in protest and journeyed on to Iconium. Luke records how they went into the next village "filled with joy and with the Holy Spirit" (v. 52).

"How do you shake the dust from your feet when you are expelled and at the same time journey on filled with joy and the Holy Spirit?" Ken Bailey once asked me. He went on to answer this rhetorical question himself: "Paul and Barnabas had come to that place where they recognized that certain parts of the human soil in Antioch had consistently rejected the seeds of the kingdom. The apostles were therefore at liberty to shake the dust off their feet, leave and travel to new pastures. They were still clutching the seeds of the kingdom, they were still energized by inner joy and still empowered by the Holy Spirit."

Did the Twelve ever act similarly, I wonder? Did they take seriously the sacrament of shaking the dust off their feet? Or

were they like many of today's disciples: when the seeds we
sow fall into inhospitable soil, we become riddled with self-
doubt. Did they, like many of us, castigate themselves? Was
their conversation sometimes punctuated with those phrases
that punctuate ours: "If only I'd spent more time in prayer
while I was preparing," "If only I hadn't taken so-and-so's
advice," "if only . . ."? Did they, like many of us, try to find
a scapegoat on which to pin the blame? Did they, like many
of us, turn the "if only's" outward: "if only he'd led the
worship differently," "If only the program had been more
imaginative," "If only the organizers had been more coop-
erative," "If only we had prayed more as a team . . ."? The
permutations are endless.

Worse, did they, like many of us, attempt the impossible? Did
they try to force seeds to fuse with the soil by introducing to
the scene yet another "modern" method of farming? In other
words, did they attempt to continue in their own strength a
task that God was clearly calling them to leave? Were they
reluctant to move on in response to God's call out of fear that
they might lose face by doing so?

Jesus anticipated such self-questioning, such self-condem-
nation and such finger-pointing. That is why he exposed the
real culprit: unreceptive soil. When the seed fails to germinate
and grow and blossom and bear fruit, the problem lies, he
insists, not with the sower and not with the seed, but with
the soil.

Did the Twelve really hear and heed his warning? Do we?

The Sacrament of Waiting
Perhaps the "sacrament of waiting"[2] is easier for the disciples
to grasp than the sacrament of failure. These men live close to
the land. They know what happens to a seed when it is
embedded in the soil. They know that it goes through an
"in-between" time when the shell disintegrates but no plant

emerges. They know that it takes time for roots to worm their way into the earth; that it takes even longer for shoots to make their upward climb. They know they must expect "first the stalk, then the head, then the full kernel in the head" (Mk 4:28). They watch such gradual, mysterious, steady growth every spring. It is a part of their culture. Can they translate these concepts to spiritual growth in people? Admittedly they don't suffer from the handicaps twentieth-century Westerners suffer from. They have never been part of a culture that clamors for everything *now*. They are not familiar with the world of instant coffee, instant credit-card currency, spontaneous telephone shopping, super-fast faxes (the list is endless). Perhaps, then, they are mercifully protected from the "quick-fix spirituality"[3] that bedevils today's church. Perhaps it is easier for them to give assent to Jesus' insistence that the growth of a soul is as slow and gradual as the germination of a seed and the ripening of its fruit.

First the seed fuses with the soil and the soil with the seed. The transition between this fusion and the plant that waves in the wind and boasts plump, ripe ears of grain is a long one. Does this help them make sense of what is currently happening in their own souls? Possibly. After all, these men were in transition themselves. They were evolving from fishermen to fishers of men.

And as they ponder the need for patience, are they entrusted with another insight? Do they see what we Westerners grasp only with difficulty—that the sacrament of waiting can be painful for another reason? The thing or person caught up in the waiting game does not act. They are acted upon—like the soil in which the sower's seed falls. The sun and the rain work on it. So does the farmer. He plows it, harrows it and fertilizes it. The soil, in turn, acts on the seed of the Word. Will the Twelve be able to translate this principle to people-in-the-making when they pastor new converts to Christianity? Can they

see that they are being acted upon by Jesus and his teaching?
Possibly. People of the land here in the Middle East, I find, gain
in innate wisdom what they sometimes lack in sophistication.
They often amaze me with their ability to get to the heart of
things in one easy step.

And we who stand at the back of the band of men; have we
heard the need to be patient—as patient with people as God is?
Have we learned "the sacrament of waiting"?

The Assurance of Harvest

Can we, like these men, believe Jesus' guarantee that there will
be a bumper harvest eventually? Perhaps they sit more comfort-
ably with this assurance than we do. After all, some of these
disciples are fishermen by trade. They might stay out in their
boats all night and catch nothing. That doesn't dishearten
them. There's always tomorrow—at least in the Middle East.
These men live close to the land. They see what happens every
year. Some crops fail and everyone bewails the loss loudly. But
if the grape harvest is poor, the chances are that the orange
harvest will be plentiful; if the carob harvest is disappointing,
the olive harvest could become a cause for rejoicing. The fig
trees may not bear fruit, but the wheat fields may well be golden
with grain.

Can we who stand at the back of that bunch of leaders-in-
the-making tune in again to Jesus' assurance: "The fields . . .
are ripe for harvest" (Jn 4:35)? Can we be reenergized by the
revelation Jesus gave to John? It describes the end of time:

> I looked and there before me was a great multitude that no
> one could count, from every nation, tribe, people and lan-
> guage, standing before the throne and in front of the Lamb.
> They were wearing white robes and were holding palm
> branches in their hands. . . . [They] serve [God] day and
> night in his temple; and he who sits on the throne will spread
> his tent over them. Never again will they hunger; never again

will they thirst. The sun will not beat upon them, nor any scorching heat. For the Lamb at the center of the throne will be their shepherd; he will lead them to springs of living water. And God will wipe away every tear from their eyes. (Rev 7:9, 15-17)

FOUR

PRAYING
THE PARABLE OF
THE SOWER

W*hen we read or hear a story or watch a film, we almost* always meditate on it. By this I mean that we turn it over and over in our minds. (According to the psalmist, this is what meditation really is.) We might also feast on it or let our feelings engage it. As we discussed earlier, that is part of the power of the parable. But as we saw in chapter three, Jesus wants more than meditation. He wants a response. He yearns that the kingdom seeds he continues to scatter be welcomed. One task that remains, therefore, is to make our own response to the parable of the sower. The questions "How am I responding?" and "How soft and deep and clean and weed-free is my heart?" can best be answered by *praying* the parable. This chapter is devoted to exploring some of the ways the Sower can form a springboard for our prayer.

Watching an Action Replay

Before meditating on the story, do some or all of the following:

☐ Find a place where you can relax and be comfortable.

☐ Recognize that God is there.

☐ Tune into his presence.

☐ Hand over to him the pressures that would prevent you from praying: any hurts and anxieties, excitements and plans.

☐ Have beside you a Bible, a pen, and a notebook or prayer journal.

☐ Ask God to give you God-blessed eyes and a Spirit-softened heart.

Now reread the story of the sower from Matthew 13:1-9 or Luke 8:1-8. After you have done this, close your eyes and invite Jesus to retell the story just for you today. As the story unfolds, listen to the details, the tone of voice and the mannerisms of the storyteller. Pay particular attention to your response.

I sometimes do this as I walk near my home. One occasion stands out in my memory. I was standing on a favorite prayer spot of mine. To my right was an expanse of freshly plowed land in which newly sown seeds were just beginning to give evidence of growth. To my left stretched an expanse of liquid-gold water framed by a mass of mountains and a sky that had been set on fire by the setting sun. I spotted one solitary fishing boat out at sea. As I stood gazing on God's grandeur, it was as though Jesus sat in that boat, retelling the story just for me. I listened as though I were hearing it for the first time. I listened not just to his words, but to the longings of his heart. I listened not just to the sequence of events, but to the language of creation. I listened, too, to the stirrings of my own emotions. I listened and listened and marveled and marveled like this for some thirty minutes.

At the beginning of that prayer walk, while I had been hiking the paths, I had been listening on my Walkman to a session Ken Bailey and I had once had on this particular parable. Ken had used a recurring phrase that was echoing through the corridors of my mind and my heart: "deep, clean, soft soil."

So after listening to Jesus retell the story, I switched the tape on, expecting to hear more from Ken. I had forgotten that while I had been standing in my prayer place, I had changed the tape. To my astonishment, I heard not Ken Bailey's voice but a most moving rendering of a familiar chorus that was expressing precisely the murmurings of my own mind and heart:

> Purify my heart, let me be as gold and precious silver
> Purify my heart, let me be as gold, pure gold
> Refiner's fire, my heart's one desire
> Is to be holy . . .
> Ready to do your will
>
> Purify my heart, cleanse me from my sin and make me holy,
> Purify my heart, cleanse me from my sin, deep within
> Refiner's fire, my heart's one desire
> Is to be holy . . .
> Ready to do your will[1]

To my amazement, tears began to course down my face—tears of longing, tears of love, tears of lament. And I found myself spontaneously echoing the prayer of the psalmist: "Create in me a pure heart, O God, and renew a steadfast spirit within me" (Ps 51:10).

This memorable, unsought, undeserved, God-graced moment handed me the key to praying this particular parable. The key, as we have already seen, is to remember that Jesus almost always leaves his parables unfinished. He leaves his listeners on a cliffhanger with the challenge to finish the story for themselves. We round a parable off with our own response. We can round this parable off with a personal response to a specific question: "Will I be receptive to God's seeds that are being scattered on the soil of my life?"

Rewriting the Story

With this in mind, another method of praying the parable suggests itself. We can pray it by rewriting Jesus' story in our own words. Keeping the story in its cultural context, we record it as though we are telling it to someone who has never heard it before. Instead of leaving the parable with a ragged ending, however, we round it off with our own heart response. When I did this on one occasion, this is what I wrote:

A sower once set out from his simple home clutching a bag of seed in one hand and a large, round, flat basket in the other. Walking away from his village, he came eventually to terraced farmland that had been cut out of the hillside. With a deftness that displayed his fitness, he negotiated the steep terrain and the stone walls and stood, at last, at the edge of his pride and joy: his own freshly tilled strip of land. The rain-soaked soil lay fallow and furrowed, ready for the spring planting. Taking his basket, the sower filled it with the seeds before walking the length and breadth of his sun-kissed patch of land. With joy and generosity he scattered handfuls of the seed hither and thither—along the side of the path, on the rich, deep, fertile soil, on the smattering of topsoil over underlying rock and even in the corners where the weeds flourish and reign. Every part of his piece of land, should, by rights, share in the forthcoming harvest.

Taking his hand-held oxen-drawn plow, the sower covered the seed with soil and then went into the prolonged period of necessary waiting. He waited and waited and waited and watched and watched and watched until, one day, he detected signs that the soil had been disturbed. It was as though particles of soil underground had been prized apart. Not long afterward a green haze seemed to hover over the terrace—a beautiful green veil that seemed pregnant with the promise of new life. That new life gradually emerged in the form of seedlings pushing their way toward the light.

The sower would go often to his piece of land where, after some months, he would pause to ponder the picture: some seed, it seemed, had produced prolific growth. The blond wheat waved in the breeze that blew in off the sea. Some seeds had obviously had a struggle to survive, and others had shriveled up in the scorching sun.

The sower felt pangs of grief when he saw the shallow, weed-ridden soil. Each separate seed he had scattered there had contained a blade of wheat: life that had been aborted. At the same time he felt full of joy as he feasted his eyes on the harvest that was soon to be reaped.

As I adventured with that sower onto his land, as I, too, scrutinized the results of his handiwork, the soil of my heart began to speak: "Send your Spirit, heavenly Sower, into every particle of the soil of my life. Soften it, cleanse it, fertilize it, deepen it, break up the clods, pull out the weeds that I may yield not just a meager harvest but fruit in abundance for you and your kingdom."

No one can write the ending of a parable for another. Each person must internalize and personalize the parable for themselves. Rewriting the story in that simple way can bring us right to the heart of things—to *today's* answer to the unspoken question Jesus asks: "Will you receive, reject or strangle the seed I'm planting in you?"

Before reading further, you might wish to pray. You could use either of the prayer exercises I have outlined so far: letting Jesus retell the story for you for today and recording in your journal the response of your heart, or retelling the story as though for someone else—then recording openly and honestly Jesus' unspoken question: "Will you receive, reject or strangle the seed I'm planting in you?"

Stepping into the Story

A third way to pray this parable is to do what the children do in one of the books in C. S Lewis's Chronicles of Narnia—*The Voyage of the Dawn Treader.* The children are in the attic of their uncle's home. On the wall hangs a picture of a boat. As they admire the picture, the boat begins to move to the rhythm of the now-surging sea. Instinctively, they climb into the ship and find themselves at the beginning of a life-changing adventure.

Surely, when the prophet Nathan told the story that melted David's heart, David stepped into the poor man's sandals in a similar way. Was it not Nathan's intention that he should do so? Was it not the resulting emotions that prompted David's outburst: "The man who did this deserves to die!" (2 Sam 12:6)? Just as David appears to have done this with Nathan's parable, so there is value in giving ourselves permission to do something similar with Jesus' parables—not simply listening to them or picturing them in our mind's eye, but stepping into them.

We might place ourselves in the sandals of the sower, for example, and go to the terrace to broadcast the seed that is so full of potential. That way we might enter into some of the sower's emotions and expectations and dreads. Or we might "become" the rocky ground, the weed-matted terrain, the soil along the path or the good ground: the soil that welcomes the fusion of the seed, the soil and the plant that together produces fruit. We might even "become" a seed falling from a sower's hands into the kind of terraced terrain Jesus envisioned, registering our reactions when we discover which part of the terrace we have landed in. Alternately we might "become" the entire terrace.

Is this not what Jesus expected his disciples to do when he made that profound statement: "I am the Vine, you are the branches. When you're joined with me and I with you, the relation intimate and organic, the harvest is sure to be abundant" (Jn 15:4)?[2]

For me, at any rate, standing at the edge of a vineyard, staring at the leprous-looking stump of the vine, marveling at the gracefulness of grape-laden branches, it seems natural to "become" a branch. It seems natural to sense how it feels to be attached to the parent. Equally, it seems natural to feel how useless I would become if I broke away or if I were amputated from God, the source of my life.

Similarly, there is a naturalness, at least for certain personality types, in engaging in a similar way with this story of the sower—seeing every aspect of it as God's finger beckoning us to receive him.

I think, for example, of an occasion when, in my prayer, I "became" a seed that fell among weeds. I remember leaving the spaciousness of the basket and the tenderness of the sower's hands only to find myself arriving in my new home—a chaotic cluster of deeply embedded roots. There seemed no place for me to be, no room for me to move, little sustenance for me to draw on. I didn't die. I more than survived. I grew. But the constant cry on my lips was "You're choking me . . . You're strangling me!!" It was both a frightening and a salutary experience. When embarking on this meditation, I was acutely aware that there is a sense in which I cannot "become" the seed scattered by the sower in Jesus' story. That seed is the Word of God, and that I can never become. By identifying with a falling seed, however, and finding myself choked, even strangled, I was reminded in a powerful way that the Word of God needs time, space and sustenance if it is to survive and thrive in a person's soul. Once again I finished the parable with a prayer that arose partly from the bitterness of the experience of the moment and partly from Jesus' own interpretation of the parable:

Forgive me, dear Sower,
for allowing roots of anger and bitterness
to threaten and restrict,
even choke and strangle

your freshly sown seed.
Forgive me that the weeds of worry,
the pressure of a thousand things to do,
the tyranny of the telephone
and the demon of disappointment
have denied your seed the nourishment it needs.
Weed me, Lord.
Re-create in me a heart that is ready
    at all times
to receive your seed
    in whatever shape or form it comes.
Grant me the further grace
    to bear fruit for your kingdom
        and your glory.

Again, you might benefit most from pausing at this point rather than reading on. As you pause, become still, seek a fresh anointing of God's Spirit, especially the grace of a Spirit-anointed imagination. Reread the parable, recalling its cultural context, then step into it at whatever point seems right for you for today. See how the story unfolds as you "become" the sower or the soil, a seed or a weed, the rocky ledge, a ravenous bird or that narrow, hard-baked thoroughfare.

When this part of your prayer is completed, again record what you have seen and sensed and heard and felt in your prayer journal. Let it give rise to a prayer of response. Then listen in case God has other things to whisper to you or other ways of enlightening you.

Such enlightenment might come as you journal, as it did for me when I "became" a seed whose life was being stifled. If you become a weed that is choking a struggling seedling, for example, you might gain a more vivid picture of ways in which the weeds in Jesus' story, "the cares of this world," overwhelm and stultify the Christian. If you "become" rock-hard ground or soil matted with weeds, you might feel overcome with helplessness as you recognize your need of Someone to come to the rescue: Someone to chip away at the rock and replace it with deep, clean soil; Someone to remove the tap roots of weeds; Someone to give you the indispensable gift of grace.

Some Spiritual Stock-Taking

"It's no good. I just don't have an imagination." That's what people sometimes say to me. If you are one of those people, remember two things. You do have an imagination, and there are ways of being reconnected with it. I have written about this elsewhere.[3] Not everyone, however, finds it helpful to engage their imagination in prayer. You might therefore find it more profitable to approach your prayer in a slightly different way.

Embarking on what I call spiritual stock-taking, for example, relies less on the imagination and more on the mind. This is one way of doing it:

□ Try to find a quiet place where you can think reflectively and where you won't be disturbed.

□ Focus your attention on the God who has promised to be with us at all times.

□ Read the parable in the way it is recorded in the Gospels.

□ Keep it in its cultural context.

□ Look at Jesus' own interpretation of it. (Mt 13:18-23; Mk 4:15-20; Lk 8:11-15).

□ Be aware that the heavenly Sower strides daily across the terrace of our hearts. Moment by moment, he scatters the seeds of the kingdom.

□ Ask the Holy Spirit to suggest to you how you might most honestly answer the following questions:

1. What kind of soil fills the terrace of my life?

2. Do precious seeds lie exposed on the untilled corners of my life?

3. Are they in danger of being snatched from me because of busyness or distractions, or for any other reason?

4. Does shallow topsoil in my life mean that seeds growing there will need special nurturing and, when the time is ripe, transplanting? If so, what does this mean in practice?

5. Where and what are the weeds in my life? Jesus names some of the weeds that strangle the life out of infant plants. Are others obstructing the Spirit in my life?

6. Are some seeds already multiplying—thirtyfold, sixtyfold and even a hundredfold? If so, where? (If you don't know, ask the Holy Spirit to show you.)

7. Can I rejoice in the soft, deep, clean soil in my soul that is producing fruit? Can I rejoice in all that is happening there?

□ Compare your response with the reaction Jesus yearned for—that the soil should receive the seed with gratitude, interact with it and bear fruit when the time was ripe.

□ Record in your journal the insights that came to you. Draw or paint a picture as your response. Or let them give rise to a prayer or a poem, like this one.

The Field
We like to think of fields
being covered by waving golden corn.
Full of promise, a rich harvest
waiting to be gathered.
Or perhaps a field of yellow trumpets,
daffodils nodding quietly in the breeze.
When we think of fields we want them to be doing
something useful, like ourselves;
or looking good, like ourselves;
or being fruitful, like ourselves.
After all, this is the aim and purpose of Christian living.
So it's rather odd, that God seems to like bare fields, lying
fallow, no crops growing,
nothing useful or pretty.
How strange that such barren wastes
should be so blessed by God.

When I asked why, a worm replied.
"'Tis what the eye cannot see that counts."
"Pardon?" I said.
"Good crops need rich soil," muttered the worm
as he burrowed back into the earth.
"Come and see," he called.
"I can't, I'm too big," I protested.
"Lie down and look with your heart," invited the worm.
So I did. I saw a field from underneath.
Perhaps God is upside down!
It was like the busiest factory or most crowded street
I've ever seen.
Creatures burrowing, scuttling, chewing, moving earth.
Millions of droplets of moisture
trickling through crevices of soil.
Cool, quiet, damp places where tiny miracles occurred.
The ears of my heart heard the field sigh
with deep contentment.
"No grass to grow nor seeds to nourish.
It is good to take a Sabbath-rest."
I strained to hear another sound, mild and gentle
like a hushed whisper. A sound I longed to hear.
"Be still, be at ease, then you will know that I am your God."
—Wendy Ward

Focus on the Person of the Sower

One valuable way of praying the parable is to focus on the person of the sower. As we saw in chapter three, the sower in the story is neither stingy nor overbearing. He is full of generosity and grace—sowing seeds in soil that is unprepared and unreceptive. As we also saw, this was not the image of God that had been presented either to the Twelve or to the devout Jew. On the contrary, they had been given an image of a formidable God. When a person is presented with a false impression of

God, her prayer life is automatically affected. If God is a tyrant whose demands seem to be unrealistic and unreasonable, she will fear him, perhaps run from him, maybe attempt to obey him in a halfhearted kind of way, but she will not find within herself the freedom to respond to God in the way his love deserves. Yet many of us today, despite our familiarity with the Gospels, have imbibed an image of God that causes us to recoil from him rather than be magnetized by his goodness.

I was reminded of this in a powerful way while writing this very paragraph. While I was tapping the keys of my computer, the telephone rang. I picked up the receiver and realized that someone was wanting to send a fax, so I pressed the start button on my fax machine and continued to type. When I heard the machine cut the page, I swiveled around in my chair, removed the page from the machine and found not a letter as I expected, but a powerful, horrific picture entitled "The Angry Christ." Underneath it were three more pictures labeled "The Protestant, the Historic and the Catholic Christ." The Protestant Christ looked as unapproachable and severe as many a stained-glass-window saint. The Catholic Christ wore a crown of thorns and looked too pathetic to be of any use to anyone. The historic Christ looked like an unkempt terrorist. The caption underneath these pictures was "Will the *Real* Christ Please Ascend."

I was still staring at these images of Jesus when another page squeezed through my fax machine. This time, the caricature of Christ came in the form of a naked woman hanging on a cross. Underneath that was a picture of a screaming Christ. The next picture followed quickly. It portrayed "Jesus the Fool." Underneath it was a message from the sender: "Hi, Joyce, I thought you might find some of these pictures interesting." Then came the final page: a picture of the thorn-crowned Christ smoking a cigarette.

As I held these pictures in my hand and gazed at them in turn, I gasped at the timing of their arrival. They reminded me

of some of the false images of God that cause people to recoil
from him today.

"Who do you say that I am?" a voice whispered as I sat at
my desk. The question was reminiscent of the time when Jesus
asked his disciples: "Who do people say that I am? Who do *you*
say that I am?" (Mt 16:13-15). Steeped as I was at that moment
in the parable of the sower and acutely aware that in describing
the sower, Jesus is painting a picture of himself, my spontaneous
reaction went something like this: "You've shown me . . ." I
paused before continuing. Suddenly I became aware of an ache
in my heart. "I've thrilled to your self-portrait in this story I'm
studying. Your strength, your dedication, your generosity, your
willingness to take risks, your patience, your understanding all
attract me to you." I paused again and gazed out of my study
window. The mountains and the Mediterranean, the vineyards
and the olive groves stared back at me. "And you're magnifi-
cent," I stuttered. "You must be since you created such a
wonderful world."

I turned from contemplating creation to contemplate the
pictures on my desk. The ache in my heart intensified. Tears
welled up within me and overflowed. Restless, I wandered
down to my garden. The tranquillity triggered more tears. Tears
are a language. They express sentiments that are too deep for
words, so I cannot hope to express precisely the prayer these
tears were uttering. All I know is that I was overwhelmed with
sorrow that though Jesus came at such great cost to himself, to
scatter kingdom seeds into the hearts of the people he loves, so
many of these people remain blind to the truth. Because they
have never encountered the true God, the God of the Scriptures, they mock him, they fabricate images of him that keep
them and others from him. I sensed that the ache in my heart
was but a pale reflection of the ache in the Sower's own heart.
It gave rise to a further prayer: that God would continue to
pour out his grace on people whose image of him is warped and

distorted. I prayed for myself, too, that the Holy Spirit would continue to show me where my image of God is inaccurate.

As I wrote my reflections in my journal, I found myself completing Jesus' story of the sower for myself, opening myself to be further equipped for the ministry of proclaiming the good news in ways others can understand.

Praying with Mental Pictures

The occasion I describe is not the only time a parable has given birth to the prayer of intercession and petition. I find that praying the parables often opens the door to praying for others as well as opens a window to the prayer of petition, praying for myself. The imagery Jesus chooses is so powerful that if we take the time to dwell on it and pray with it, it can prompt one prayer after another.

When praying the parables, some people like to have a visual focus in the place where they pray: a candle or a picture, an ear of wheat or a seed. When the parable of the sower is to form the basis of your prayer, it might be helpful, in addition to these visual aids, to hold in your mind a mental picture that arises out of the story as Jesus told it: the sower scattering his seed, a single seed falling to the ground, the path connecting one strip of land to another, the weed-riddled patch and so on.

Focus on that picture for several minutes. As you do so it will probably evolve—the seed might begin to sprout, for example. Extract from the sequence of changes whatever seems to be profitable for this early phase of your prayer. Recall the cultural context of the story and the mindset of the people to whom Jesus first told it. Ask the Holy Spirit to baptize your imagination and to open the eyes and ears of your heart. Listen attentively to the conversation you are having with yourself and to the language of your emotions as well as to Jesus' story. Let prayer pour from you in whatever way it chooses: through intercession, petition, adoration, wonder, spiritual warfare, tears, groans, deep-down silence. Record what happened in your journal and write your own ending to the parable of the sower as you would want to update it for today.

I remember praying in this way on one occasion when I imagined the mystery of the movement that takes place underneath the soil when the seed and the soil begin to interact with each other. First of all I imagined small cracks appearing in the shell of the seed, then a small shoot pushing its head into the beckoning soil. Suddenly, into my mind came the names of people known to me who are experiencing a similar sense of disorientation—people in transition. I thought of a certain group of teenagers—neither children nor adults—who, like an emerging plant, are somewhere in between. They face the challenge of allowing the seed of God's Word to fuse with their emotions and attitudes and wills and relationships so that in time they might bear more fruit for the kingdom. They had invited my husband and me to meet with them to discuss how they could best negotiate these in-between years. I thought too of a friend who is having a midlife crisis and who seems more conscious of the disorientation she is experiencing as God's Word fuses with the soil of her soul than of the potential fruit she will yield when the plant of her life matures and ripens even more. I held these and others like them into the encircling love of God.

On another occasion, when I prayed with Jesus' symbols of the disintegrating seed fusing with the soil and giving birth to new life, the mental pictures engendered quite a different prayer. This time I seemed to see the seed and the soil and the plant being acted on in a different way. On this occasion I found myself interceding for a friend suffering through a particularly painful transition. She was undergoing that bewildering part of the spiritual pilgrimage some call "the wilderness experience" and others "the dark night of the soul." This is the stage of the journey where we discover that, by and large, we no longer take the initiative—not even in prayer. We rediscover, often through pain and frustration, that God is the initiator of our faith. We love only because he loved us first. This friend, like most of us when we enter the wilderness, was finding it almost impossible to accept that "when you're waiting, you're *not* doing nothing. You're doing the most important something there is. You're allowing your soul to grow up. If you can't be still and wait, you can't become what God created you to be."⁴ And so my heart enfolded her. Having held her into God's love as well as my own, I prayed then that I might continue to learn the lessons of the desert; that I might be receptive to the changes he is wanting to make in me.

Praying with Images of Failure

According to Jesus' story, some seeds may never germinate and grow. Whenever we expend time and energy on sowing kingdom seeds, we run the risk of rejection and failure. We might therefore find ourselves drawn to pray with the images of failure Jesus paints in this parable: the seed being carried away in the beak of a bird, the seedling being shriveled up by the sun, the young plant being strangled by the thorns.

Or again, leaning less heavily on our imagination and intuition and more on our mind, we might benefit from taking Jesus' provision of "a sacrament of failure" as the starting point for our prayer. We might find ourselves inspired to pray for individuals known to us who are suffering much pain—like the Christians working overseas who once confessed to me that they were tempted to give up. They worked in a country where time and money and personnel had been poured in for years. "But look at the fruit," they groaned. "It's pathetic. We're wasting our time and money and energy."

Or our prayer might be more general or more personal: more general in that we simply fold into God's embrace any who are suffering silently, or more personal because we pray for our own fears of failure. The prayer for ourselves might include a longing that God would give us the grace to fathom that deep mystery he spreads before us through Isaiah: that our ways are not God's ways, nor are God's ways our ways. God's ways are higher than our ways. This prayer might also take on board the realization that this prophet who was the mouthpiece through whom God poured these consoling words was the prophet whose ministry was doomed to failure from the beginning. As Dame Maria Boulding expresses it: "At the core of Isaiah's call was the reminder that the response to his work would be one of the hardening of hearts and a gnawing disinterest among the people."[5]

Visual Aids

Just as it is possible to take each of Jesus' word-pictures and to let these inspire our prayer, so it is possible to take, one by one, each of the deep, theological truths he is spelling out in this parable and to let that trigger a series of prayers.

Some people, however, find it most helpful to pray with an actual visual aid rather than an imaginary or mental one. For this reason I'll conclude this chapter by describing two such visual aids that have helped me to pray this parable.

The first is a transparent box containing sunflower seeds that currently sits in the prayer corner in my study. I planted these seeds just before beginning to write this chapter. When the seedlings sprang up in the seed tray, they came wearing comical "hats"—the shell of the seeds from which their life had emerged. I gently lifted the "hats" off their heads and placed them in this see-through box. Some seeds look as though the plant they contained burst out of them in a flurry of energetic exuberance that broke and disfigured the parent seed. Others look as though the seedling slipped out quietly, almost unobtrusively. The slit in their side seems scarcely noticeable.

I sometimes lift one seed or another from the box, finger it, gaze at it and marvel that one small shell like this can contain so much potential. The experience often gives rise to a prayer that I may continually be receptive to every seed God implants in me. At other times, as I look at the seed before me, I find myself praying that when God gives me the privilege of sowing kingdom seeds in people's hearts, I may become more conscious that these seeds are precious, potentially life-giving and life-changing. This fills me with awe at the sheer privilege of being entrusted with the task of seed sowing. It also humbles me.

My second visual aid came to me like a gift from God himself. I woke before sunrise one morning while I was writing this chapter to discover that the farmer who owns the field opposite our home had spent the night gathering in the harvest. Neat bales of hay studded his land. For two days, the picture of fruitfulness lay framed by my bedroom window. For two days it inspired my prayer. Then the laborers returned. I watched them heave one bundle after another onto the waiting truck. They continued right through the heat of the day. As they secured their precious cargo with a coil of rope, I wondered how they felt. Hot, no doubt. Thirsty, no doubt. Exhausted, no doubt. And, if my interpretation of their excited cries was accurate, exultant also. My mind sped into fast forward as I looked to that last and final harvest when the heavenly Sower will reap the rewards of the seeds he has sown. The scene before me and the anticipation that flooded my heart drew from me yet another prayer. Like many of our most heartfelt prayers, it was wordless. Just a silent but profound feeling of awe and wonder.

Even so, come, Lord Jesus.

THE PARABLE
OF THE
GOOD SAMARITAN

On one occasion an expert in the law stood up to test Jesus. "Teacher,"
he asked, "what must I do to inherit eternal life?"

"What is written in the Law?" he replied. "How do you read it?"

He answered: " 'Love the Lord your God with all your heart
and with all your soul
and with all your strength and with all your mind'; and,
'Love your neighbor as yourself.' "

"You have answered correctly," Jesus replied. "Do this and you will live."

But he wanted to justify himself, so he asked Jesus,
"And who is my neighbor?"

In reply Jesus said: "A man was going down from Jerusalem
to Jericho, when he fell into the hands of robbers.
They stripped him of his clothes, beat him and went away, leaving
him half dead. A priest happened to be going down
the same road, and when he saw the man, he passed by on the
other side. So too, a Levite, when he came to
the place and saw him, passed by on the other side. But a Samaritan,
as he traveled, came where the man was;
and when he saw him, he took pity on him. He went to him and
bandaged his wounds, pouring on oil and wine.
Then he put the man on his own donkey, took him to an inn
and took care of him. The next day he took out
two silver coins and gave them to the innkeeper.
'Look after him,' he said, 'and when I return,
I will reimburse you for any extra expense you may have.'

"Which of these three do you think was a neighbor to the man
who fell into the hands of robbers?"

The expert in the law replied, "The one who had mercy on him."

Jesus told him, "Go and do likewise."

LUKE 10:25-37

FIVE

UNDERSTANDING THE PARABLE OF THE GOOD SAMARITAN

M*any of Jesus' parables are like symphonies with four* movements. The first movement captures our attention with the story line. The second movement presents us with a pattern for living that shows how a citizen of the kingdom might be expected to flesh out his or her faith ethically. The third movement hands us some kingdom secrets—Jesus' theology in a nutshell. The finale brings the story to a climax by highlighting the nature or ministry of the King himself.

Ken Bailey claims that many of Jesus' parables also seem to have been designed to underline four major theological thrusts that can best be summarized with a diagram:

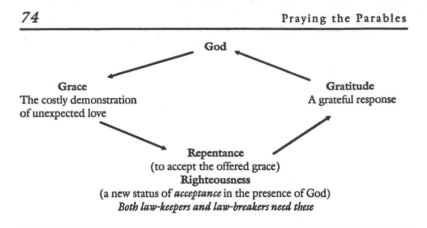

Four major thrusts in the theology of Jesus

All things begin with God. In his mercy, God has come to us with an offer of unexpected love. His advent took the form of Jesus. His costly demonstration of love expresses itself in many forms. The climax of that love is reached on the cross of Calvary.

Jesus' love is poured out onto two categories of sinners: law-breakers and law-keepers. Each is worse than the other. Law-keepers easily fall into the trap of believing they do not need an offer of love because they keep every jot and tittle of the law. Scores of law-breakers, on the other hand, think they are so worthless that the love so freely offered cannot possibly be for them. Even so, law-breakers are often more ready to accept Jesus' undeserved love than the self-contained law-keepers who are determined to earn acceptance with God in their own way. Jesus put the situation memorably. Addressing a bunch of law-keepers, he threw out this challenge: "I tell you that crooks and whores are going to precede you into God's kingdom. John came to you showing you the right road. You turned up your noses at him, but the crooks and whores believed him. Even when you saw their changed lives, you didn't care enough to change and believe him" (Mt 21:32 The Message).

The act of faith Jesus refers to is called *repentance*. The one repenting receives many good gifts, including a new status in

the eyes of God. This is *righteousness.* Rightness with God.
People on the receiving end of the divine love find welling up
within themselves the urge to make a response—the response
of heartfelt gratitude. This process is so life-changing that,
understandably, attempts are often made to condense it into a
doctrine. In doing so, the impression is sometimes given that
salvation is not by grace but by formula. "Accept this list of
ideas with your mind and conform to this code of behavior with
your will and peace with God and salvation will be yours."
Succeeding generations then face the danger of obeying a list
of dos and don'ts rather than embarking on the adventure of
responding to grace.

The Pharisees had fallen into this trap. For them, the law was
not an expression of gratitude to God for grace received. The
law had become the means by which the "righteous," the
law-keepers, and the "unrighteous," the law-breakers, could be
easily detected. The way to become righteous, in their eyes, was
to repent of having broken the law and to pledge yourself to
keeping it.

Jesus consistently wages war with this philosophy by insisting
that true righteousness involves acceptance of a gift that triggers
a response of love to Love. He consistently calls on his listeners
to make an act of true repentance by responding to the costly
demonstration of love that he came to give. His story of the
good Samaritan calls for a response of this nature.

Putting the Parable in Context

As we have already observed, if we are to extract the flavor from
a parable, so far as we are able, we must place that story in its
historical and cultural context. As we have also discovered, one
way of doing this is to stand or sit at the back of the group of
people to whom Jesus first told the parable and listen and watch,
learn and discern by receiving the story through their eyes. This
is what we will now attempt to do with this memorable story.

To do this, it would appear that we will probably have to sit with a group of Pharisees and teachers of the law. Luke doesn't tell us whether others are present. But he does tell us that this story is triggered by a lawyer's question.

Listen while the lawyer puts the question to Jesus. As is customary in the Middle East, he, the student, stands and addresses Jesus as "Teacher," Luke's word for rabbi. Notice that he's giving a mixed message, however. His lips and body language are expressing respect for Jesus. His heart, on the other hand, desires to trip Jesus up (Luke 10:25).

Jesus fields the lawyer's question skillfully. Instead of answering it, in true Middle Eastern fashion he responds to the question with another question. The lawyer asks: "Teacher, what must I do to inherit eternal life?" whereupon Jesus appeals to his questioner's profession by asking: "What does the law demand, as you understand it?" A clever return. Jesus knows full well that any lawyer will affirm a response that implies, "Keep the law."

Jesus could have put the lawyer down by pointing out that the question has a simple answer. No one can do anything to inherit anything. Inheritance, by its very nature, is a gift. Jesus chose not to go down that route but rather to play the lawyer at his own game.

To his credit, the lawyer quotes a known summary of the law that may originate with Jesus himself (cf. Mt 22:37-40), and answers: "Love the Lord your God with all your heart and with all your soul and with all your strength and with all your mind," and "Love your neighbor as yourself" (Lk 10:27). The genius of this reply is that the lawyer places love for God before love for neighbor even though these two commands come in the reverse order in the Old Testament. There, love for neighbor is listed in Leviticus and love for God in Deuteronomy. But as Ken Bailey underlines, "it is only through the love of God that the believer is to approach the people."[1]

The repartee continues with Jesus' quick-witted response: "Do this and you will live." The response takes the wind out of the lawyer's sails. He knows it's impossible for anyone to fulfill all those demands all the time. Instead of leveling with Jesus with an honest response, "It's impossible!" Luke tells us that he wanted to justify himself, so he asked another question. "He wanted to justify himself." Does this mean he wants to save face? Or to find a loophole? Or does it mean that to give his question its full theological weight, although he wants to be accepted by God (which is what justification means), he is determined to save himself by his own efforts? If he is going to justify himself before God by his own efforts, he must have some definitions. So he persists: "Who is my neighbor?"

Sly smiles creep across the faces of some of the crowd at this point. The lawyer, they see, is in rare form. He really is putting Jesus to the test, because this very question is currently the subject of debate by the teachers of the law.

If the lawyer is in rare form, so is Jesus. Into their debate he drops a seemingly simple story: "A man was going down from Jerusalem to Jericho, when he fell into the hands of robbers . . ." They're hooked. They can picture the scene in their mind's eye. They know that road well. For seventeen dangerous miles it snakes through hot and hostile desert. The route is a notorious haunt for hijackers. They picture the horrific scene: one solitary man, whom they assume to be a Jew, being mugged, stripped, robbed and dumped, half-murdered, by the side of the road.

We twentieth-century listeners must be aware, at this point in the story, of certain insinuations and innuendos that our companions in the crowd are picking up. The phrase "half dead" that Jesus uses is rabbinic shorthand for "unconscious." (The rabbis had four categories of ailing people: sick, very sick, half dead and dead.) In their mind's eye, the people in the audience are visualizing a man lying unconscious and naked in the middle of this terrifying terrain. The victim's loss of consciousness and his nakedness are bad news for reasons that will soon become apparent.

The Priest
Let Jesus continue: "A priest happened to be going down the same road, and when he saw the man, he passed by on the other side" (v. 31). Our companions know that priests are members of the upper class of their society. From this they will assume that the priest will not be walking but will be riding. Ken Bailey explains:

In the Middle East no one with any status in the community takes seventeen-mile hikes through the desert. The poor walk. Everyone else in general, and the upper classes in particular, always ride. This is the natural assumption of the parable. The same kind of assumption prevails in the American scene when a farmer says, "I am going to town." If the destination is seventeen miles away you know he will be driving. He does not mention his car. There is no need to do so.[2]

The priest approaches the slumped body of the dying man. We twentieth-century eavesdroppers are almost begging him to stop to render first aid. We are scandalized by Jesus' comment "He passed by on the other side." "Why? Why? Why didn't he stop?" we protest. Not so our companions. They know why he didn't stop. He had five good reasons.

Ben Sirach, a famous Jewish scholar before the time of Christ, was partly responsible for one of them. He warned against helping a sinner:

If you do a good turn, know for whom you are doing it, and your good deeds will not go to waste. Do good to a devout man, and you will receive a reward, if not from him, then certainly from the Most High. . . . Give to a devout man, *do not go to the help of a sinner.* Do good to a humble man, *give nothing to a godless one.* Refuse him bread, do not give him any. . . . For the Most High himself detests sinners, and will repay the wicked with vengeance. Give to the good man and *do not go to the help of a sinner.*[3]

Is this wounded man a sinner? The priest doesn't know so he passes by on the other side.

A second reason the priest hurries on is that the area no longer feels safe. The very sight of that naked, bleeding body lying there in the dust fills the priest with a sense of urgency. The bandits who robbed and assaulted this pathetic figure might still be lurking behind a nearby rock. The priest is alone. No doubt fear adds wings to his feet and persuades him to escape while the going is good—"every man for himself." So he passes by on the other side.

Jesus' audience knows that there is another reason the priest is afraid to linger. In the Middle East, if you witness a road accident, it is unwise to become involved. If you stop, a crowd of local people may gather around you and kill you. In all probability they will accuse you of *causing* the accident. Why else would you stop? Westerners find this philosophy hard to grasp. When we do grasp it, we realize that this is a possible third reason the priest passed by on the other side.

There is a fourth reason the priest chose to ignore the dying man. Leviticus 19:18 defines the phrase "your neighbor" in this way: a neighbor is "one of your people." But who is the wounded man? How is the priest to know, as he rides closer to this battered, bleeding body, whether the man is a Jew or a Gentile? Travelers normally identify strangers in two ways: by the language or dialect they speak and by their clothing. The Middle Eastern world is full of ethnic-religious communities that each speak their own language: peasants speak Aramaic, residents of the Gaza Strip speak Ashdodic, citizens of the Sea of Galilee region speak Syriac, people in the Greek cities speak Greek, and so on. Similarly, people from various regions, even various villages, are recognizable by their distinctive clothing. If you want to know the background of a fellow traveler, you engage him in conversation for the sake of hearing his voice, and you observe his apparel.

But this half-dead man has been stripped of all his clothing and, in his unconscious state, has lost the power of speech as well. There is no way the priest can tell whether he is a fellow Jew and thus should be helped as a neighbor or whether he is a non-Jew who is not the priest's responsibility. Not only this, but the victim might be dead. If he is dead, and the priest comes within four cubits, that is, within six feet of him, the priest will defile himself. Such defilement will have far-reaching consequences. Priests collect, distribute and eat tithes. If he defiles himself, he can do none of these things. His family and servants will suffer as a result. They will not be able to eat the tithes either.

Even worse, if the priest defiles himself, he will suffer inexpressible humiliation. The crowd listening to Jesus' story is conversant with other facts that help to illuminate this story. According to the Mishnah, a collection of sayings of Jewish scholars from 200 B.C. to A.D. 200, the temple could be served by priests, Levites and laymen. Many priests in the time of Jesus lived in Jericho but went regularly to Jerusalem to do a two-week stint of temple duty. Jesus' audience is probably assuming that this priest is returning home after two weeks of leading worship in the temple. They are aware that if he defiles himself for any reason on the way home, the law requires him to return to Jerusalem, to the same temple building he has just left and to suffer the humiliation of identifying himself with the "unclean." Not only does this bring shame to the priest, but the outworking of the consequences is time-consuming and costly. The "rites of purification" will take at least one week. They dictate that before a priest can be restored, he must scour the land until he finds a red heifer. He must then buy it and burn the whole body until it is reduced to ashes.

It follows that the cost of going to the dying man is very great. Since the commandment to love one's neighbor is conditional, while the command not to defile oneself is unconditional, the priest probably feels fully justified in passing by on the other side. In fact, while we Westerners are booing "the bad guy," at least one modern British expositor steeped in the early Jewish sources affirms that Jesus' Pharisaic audience will applaud when they discover that the priest decides the laws of ceremonial purity are more important than all other regulations and duties.[4]

The Levite

"A priest happened to be going down the same road, and when he saw the man, he passed by on the other side. So too," continues Jesus, "a Levite, when he came to the place and saw him, passed by on the other side" (vv. 31-32). Levites are assistant priests. Servants. The audience knows this. They know, too, that a Levite is of a lower class than a priest. They almost certainly assume that this man is walking.

They will also assume that the Levite knows that there's a priest ahead of him. They know that the contours of this road are such that it is possible to see the way ahead for considerable distances for most of the journey. Furthermore, most travelers make it their business to discover who else is making the same tortuous journey. Their lives might depend on it.

The Levite is not bound by as many rules and regulations as the priest. It would have been possible for this man to administer first aid, and, if the victim died on his hands or if he had found him already dead, the repercussions for him would not have been as serious as for the priest. Was this the reason the Levite appears to have approached the man? ("He came to the place.") Did he cross the defilement line by coming within six feet of the victim? If so, why did he do it? Just to satisfy his curiosity with a closer look? Then why did he not help the man? Why did he too pass by on the other side? Was it because of the constant danger from robbers? That could be one reason. Ken Bailey and others believe, however, that a more subtle reason governed the Levite's behavior: that *"it is the example of the higher ranking priest that deters him."*[5] Not only can he reason with himself, *If the priest ahead did nothing, why should I, a mere Levite, trouble myself?* He can go one step further. He can persuade himself that since the priest refrained from helping the man, this must be the correct course of action. If he was to move in where the priest stayed away, by implication he would be accusing the priest of hardness of heart and criticizing the priest's interpretation of the law. What right had he, the assistant priest, to call into question the actions of his superior? So, like the priest before him, he withdrew, and like the priest, he fades from the scene. But those words of Jesus still jangle in our ears: He "passed by on the other side."

This part of the parable is so powerful, so contemporary, so disturbing that some readers might prefer to pause to pray at this point of the story rather than to rush on.

Praying This Part of the Parable
One way I sometimes do this is to grab my prayer journal and simply pour out to God the emotions that come to the surface as I meditate on this segment of the story. Having recognized afresh some of the reasons the priest and the Levite might have "passed by on the other side," I once wrote, for example:
Beloved,
I find myself profoundly shaken by this first part of the parable of the good Samaritan. How can it be that a priest could become so much a victim of a rule book that he believes so deeply that black is white? No wonder you were enraged—not with the individuals caught in the theological trap, but with the system that constitutes the trap.

The scene, I know, has so many contemporary parallels . . . I went on to list some of the parallels that sprang into my mind. You might find it helpful to do the same and to pray with your list in front of you.

On another occasion when I was praying with this part of the parable, I was convicted of the reasons I give for passing by on the other side. You also might find it helpful and salutary to ask the Holy Spirit to show you where, deliberately or unwittingly, you have refused to reach out to those God has been urging you to help.

I also find it helpful to pray the following prayer on a weekly basis. I follow it with a time of silence during which I attempt to allow God to reveal the answers he wants me to discern:

Lord,

What opportunities for serving others have you sent across my path this week? Did I respond in the way you hoped? Did I, at any stage, turn my back on injustice or oppression when you wanted me to speak or work for justice or shalom? If so, why did I do this? Was I guilty of being like the priest or the Levite?[6]

I also find there is value in reflecting on pleas like the following from time to time:

We are all God's children.
I have knocked at your door
I have called to your heart
because I dream of a soft bed
because I am eager for a well-lighted house.
Why do you drive me away?
Open to me, brother!

Why do you question me
About the shape of my nose
The thickness of my lips

The colour of my skin
The name of my gods?
Open to me, brother![7]

Prayer is developing a close relationship with God. The closer
we come to God, the more we shall catch his compassion for
the world he loves. Compassion means to share a passion. The
story so far reflects the passion Jesus felt about religious laws
that made people think that they were pleasing God when in
fact they were causing God considerable anguish. Sadly, situations like this crop up in the church and so-called Christian
communities today. Talk to God about any known to you. Let
the Holy Spirit pray through you for these situations and the
individuals who are trapped by them.

SIX

THE GOOD
SAMARITAN

When the curtain went down on the last chapter, it left
the battered, bleeding victim dying by the side of the Jerusalem-
to-Jericho road. It left the mounted priest and the Levite,
having each looked at, ignored and abandoned the sufferer,
continuing their homeward journeys. It left Jesus, by implication, paving the way to blast any religious system that handcuffs
its adherents and prevents them from incarnating the love of
God. It left the Pharisaic audience, in all probability, applauding
the choices made first by the priest and then by the Levite. It
might have left some of us deeply disturbed, even burning with
rage that religious leaders, in the name of a Holy God, could
consistently conspire to "pass by on the other side."

As the curtain rises on this second act of the drama, the
atmosphere is electric. The slumped body of the wounded man
still lies there like the remains of a dog that has been run over

by a bus. The priest continues to canter home. The Levite continues to follow on foot. The scene is clearly set for a new actor to appear.

We observed in the last chapter that three categories of people were permitted to assist with temple worship in Jerusalem: priests, Levites and laymen. The audience knows what is coming next. Or at least they think they do. A layman will come along. He does. But not the kind of layman they expect. Jesus injects shock waves into the story. *This* layman is a Samaritan.

The cold, bitter war between the Jews and the Samaritans has already raged for centuries—so much so that the Mishnah declared: "He that eats the bread of the Samaritans is like to one that eats the flesh of swine." At this moment in time, the bitterness is more intense than ever, because a few years ago some Samaritans defiled the temple during Passover. Does an audible gasp go up from the crowd when they hear the word *Samaritan?* Do they groan aloud? Or boo? That's what might well happen if someone were to tell such a story to Greek Cypriots and introduce a good Turk as the hero. Do we detect a change in the tone of Jesus' voice when he says the Samaritan, "as he traveled, came where the man was"? Does he pause for effect, to let the message sink in as he goes on: "and when he saw him, he took pity on him"?

The Samaritan was certainly riding, not walking (Lk 10:34). It is probable that he watched from afar the figures first of the priest, then of the Levite pause on this spot, ponder and then hurry on. The Samaritan came. The Samaritan saw. The Samaritan cared. The Samaritan acted. The sight of the victim filled him with compassion.

The Greek word for compassion is *splanchnizomai,* which has at its root the word meaning "innards." Roughly translated, it means "to hurt at gut level." The word is used twelve times in the New Testament—three times in parables (Mt 18:27; Lk 10:33; 15:20) and nine times to describe the depth of Jesus' concern for the sick and the bereaved, the hungry and the lost.[1]

The Samaritan feels similar compassion for the heap of humanity slumped at his feet. The crowd sitting in front of us knows that the Samaritan, though detested, is not a Gentile. Samaritans are bound by precisely the same Old Testament law as Jews are. This stranger knows that the Torah defines the word *neighbor* narrowly, confining it to a fellow countryman or kinsman, a person of one's own kind. They are in Judea. The Samaritan will naturally assume that the wounded man is a Jew. Since a Jew is not a "son of his own house" and therefore not a neighbor to the Samaritan, he could choose to do nothing. The law would not fault him. Instead, the lone rider has compassion on the victim lying by the roadside and decides that he will take action.

Jesus now paints a Mother Teresa of Calcutta kind of picture. The Samaritan goes to the dying man, takes him in his arms, and, seeing that both sides of the wounds are still bleeding, binds up the wounds in true Middle Eastern style, then pours oil and wine on them to prevent the bandage from sticking and to ensure that the healing properties reach the injuries.

The Samaritan goes further. Picture the scene. He lifts the unconscious victim onto his donkey, leads him to an inn and there continues to take care of him himself. Does the audience gasp when they hear Jesus' story rising to this crescendo? Possibly. After all, they know what twentieth-century listeners might not know—that the inn is not situated a few miles down the road in the desert or in some beautiful spot in the country-side. No one establishes an inn in the middle of the desert. One reason is that it would be unsafe to do so. Look what happened to the wounded man! In the Middle East, as in most parts of the world, inns are situated in the middle of towns. So where did the Samaritan take his patient? As Jesus continues his story, some of his listeners might be picturing the Samaritan, the donkey and the Jew traveling back uphill to Jerusalem. Others might be picturing them traveling downhill to Jericho. Jesus doesn't specify the place. His audience knows, though, that the Samaritan eventually arrives in a *Jewish* town with the bedraggled body of a bleeding *Jew* draped across his donkey.

Do the hearts of Jesus' listeners stand still as they picture the scene? Do some of them groan? Possibly. They know that the Samaritan is taking a huge risk. He could well be lynched, even killed by the inhabitants of the town—just as an Indian bringing a wounded cowboy back to town might well have been murdered in the Old West.

They know why the Samaritan must take this risk, though. They know why he doesn't leave his patient at the edge of the town and make a hasty departure before his identity is detected. Innkeepers are notorious. If a wounded man is dumped on the doorstep of an inn, the probability is that he will be beaten up yet again. This man has nothing—not even his clothes. He wouldn't be able to pay an innkeeper's bill, so instead of nursing him back to health, the innkeeper would sell him as a slave. The Samaritan knows that if his Jewish companion is to be brought back to wholeness, he himself must linger at the inn (despite the further danger to himself), care for him personally and pay the bill out of his own pocket. In a superlative demonstration of costly, sacrificial caring, this is precisely what he does. He lavishes on the injured man all the attention and care that the priest and the Levite have both neglected to give. "The Samaritan is an unknown stranger. Yet, in spite of the cost in time, effort, money and personal danger, he freely demonstrates unexpected love to the one in need."[2]

Does the victim recover? Does the Samaritan escape with his life? Or, when the Samaritan eventually leaves the inn, does he fall victim to an unruly, bloodthirsty mob clamoring for his life? Jesus doesn't tell us. Instead he lets the curtain fall on the story.

Still holding in his mind the lawyer's questions that prompted him to tell the tale in the first place—"What must I do to inherit eternal life?" "Who is my neighbor?"—Jesus now turns to the lawyer and puts to him a pertinent question: "Which of these three do you think was a neighbor to the man who fell in the hands of robbers?"

Luke now gives the lawyer the exalted title "expert in the law." The expert deliberates for himself: "The one who had mercy."

"You asked me how you could inherit eternal life," Jesus insinuates. *"You* go and do the same."

We twentieth-century listeners are in danger of hearing only a fraction of the implied meaning here. We are in danger of believing that the lawyer asks, "Who is my neighbor?" and that Jesus answers, "Anyone in need, even if he is an outsider or unknown stranger—like this wounded man." But this is not what Jesus says. Jesus refrains from answering the lawyer's question. He declines to tell the lawyer who his neighbor is. Instead he answers the unasked question, "To whom must I *become* a neighbor?" In his story, the neighbor is not the wounded man but the Samaritan. Even more radical, Jesus encourages the lawyer to revise his view of the law. "The law of Moses is good," Jesus affirms. "But love is always prepared to go beyond it. Love recognizes that good though it is, the law is not an adequate guide for determining the response of reciprocal love to the God of the covenant who loves his people and suffers to save them."

In other words, Jesus addresses the lawyer's questions on two levels. On one level he seems to be saying, "If you want to know who your neighbor is so that you can love him as you love yourself, then see *yourself* as the neighbor and reach out to anyone in need. Let the good Samaritan be your model. If, on the other hand, you really want to understand justification and the way to inherit eternal life, then recognize that *you* are the wounded one. God comes to *you* at great cost and binds up your wounds even as he promised Israel." By implication, he adds: "I am the Samaritan, and I am fleshing out that promise."

To use the language of the diagram at the beginning of the last chapter, these men in the crowd today are the law-keepers. The only way the lawyer can possibly act out Jesus' injunction is to respond to love and not merely obey the law. The lawyer himself, quoting Jesus, no doubt, has summarized the law: "Love God and love your neighbor," *in that order.* Jesus here is putting his finger right on the problem. The lawyer cannot justify himself. If he is to flesh out Jesus' instructions, to emulate the good Samaritan, to *become* a neighbor wherever and whenever God's finger beckons him to alleviate someone's need, he must receive for himself the divine love. That act of receiving is his repentance.

The Pharisaic audience no doubt realizes that Jesus is not castigating one insensitive priest or one fictitious Levite. He is condemning the idea that our duty before God can be fulfilled in its entirety by a more and more precise definition of the law. As they slink away, do these teachers of the law ponder the clear implications of this story? Do we? Do we hear that Jesus is not simply spinning a memorable yarn? He is not simply showing a lawyer and us that like the Samaritan, we must have compassion for the poor, though he is emphasizing that. He is also revealing the secrets of the King and his kingdom.

Does the lawyer discern them? He is an intelligent man. He is doubtless well versed in the Scriptures. Does he make the connections Jesus hopes that he will make? Does he realize that in very many ways Jesus is echoing the prophets? Listen to the language he selects. The Samaritan "binds up" the victim's wounds. That is precisely what God promises to do through Jeremiah: " 'I will restore you to health and heal your wounds,' declares the Lord" (30:17).

In Hosea we find God, the perfect physician, pledging himself to his people, promising to heal the torn and bind up the wounds of the injured (6:1), promising, too, to come to revive and restore his people so that they might live in his presence (6:2-3). Does the seed from which Jesus' story grew also lie embedded in this book? "As marauders lie in ambush for a man, so do bands of priests." Or, as another version puts it, "As robbers lie in wait for a man, priests . . . commit villainy" (Hos 6:9).

We have an advantage over the lawyer for whom Jesus told the story of the good Samaritan. We have the New Testament Scriptures as well as the Old Testament. We have already seen that just as the good Samaritan hurt at gut level when he saw the injured man, so we read frequently that Jesus felt "full of compassion" for people he met. But this is not the only clue we have. Other parts of the story also seem to draw parallels between the Samaritan and Jesus.

Take two little cameos, for example. First, the image of the Samaritan. He is the hated outsider. This is precisely how the Pharisees and teachers of the law perceived Jesus. Or take the language Jesus used to describe the traditional Middle Eastern way of rendering first aid. Does he select his vocabulary carefully when he used the word *pour*? Is he deliberately using the language of worship? Possibly. The priest and the Levite in the story have been pouring out oil and wine on the high altar before God during their time of ministry in the temple precincts. For centuries, however, the prophets have been stressing that God wants his people to go beyond ritual and sacrifice and to respond to his love with offerings of self-giving love.

For I desire mercy, not sacrifice, and acknowledgment of God rather than burnt offerings. (Hos 6:6)

Will the LORD be pleased with thousands of rams, with ten thousand rivers of oil? Shall I offer my firstborn for my transgression, the fruit of my body for the sin of my soul? He has showed you . . . what is good. And what does the LORD require of you? To act justly and to love mercy and to walk humbly with your God. (Mic 6:7-8)

The Samaritan acts out these requests. He pours out oil and wine, not on the altar in the temple but on the altar of a dying man's wounds. Jesus, in turn, will pour out the wine of his life-blood on the altar of our lives.

There is another little cameo within this story that points us to Jesus. Luke tells us that the Samaritan lifted the injured man onto his own donkey. The Greek text that follows can be read in two ways. It might mean that the Samaritan brought or led *him* to the inn, or it could mean that the Samaritan brought or led *it* to the inn. If we assume the second possibility, here we have a picture of a comparatively wealthy Samaritan leading a wretched, semiconscious man through the heat of the desert to an inn in a Jewish town. In other words, we have an image of the Samaritan acting out the form of a slave for the sake of the one he is determined to rescue, which is precisely what we see Jesus doing at the Last Supper and elsewhere.

Theologians in the earliest centuries consistently identified the good Samaritan with Jesus himself. Was one reason because in John's Gospel, the Jews taunt him with the insult "Aren't we right in saying that you are a Samaritan and demon-possessed?" (Jn 8:48)? Or was it because they felt from Jesus the outpouring of the costly demonstration of unexpected love that had flowed from the Samaritan? Was it also because Jesus appears suddenly and dramatically, from the outside, as it were? Was it because he saw humankind's plight and knew only too well what the religious leaders had refused to give, and so he came? Like the good Samaritan, he not only cared, he came. In fact, he overflowed with compassion. When we hurt, he hurts. And so he more than compensated for all that others had refused or neglected to do or give. Like the good Samaritan, he incarnated his compassion.

Did the lawyer realize that day that the good Samaritan was not a figment of Jesus' imagination? Did he realize that the good Samaritan and Jesus are one and the same person—that

Jesus has spelled out for him his own understanding of his mission and calling? As God's agent, he has come in the guise of a self-sacrificing servant, to save.

If he heard, what response did he make? We are not told. What we are told, by implication, is the single response Jesus begs him to make. "Receive my offer of unexpected love. Let it flow into you, free you and overflow from you to others. In this way you will inherit eternal life."

We will never know how the lawyer responded to that plea. We can never really know how anyone responds, except ourselves. That is why it is vital to finish Jesus' drama for ourselves. Like the lawyer, many of us have an internal tape that plays the persuasive message "If you are good, you will go to heaven." Jesus longs that we should switch that tape off and listen to his plaintive voice that promises we will enter his kingdom for one reason only—because Someone loves us. That Someone loves us enough to die for us so that our entrance to his kingdom is secured. One of the purposes of praying this particular parable is to discover for ourselves precisely how we are responding to Jesus' heartfelt beckoning of love. That is the aim of the next chapter.

SEVEN

PRAYING THE PARABLE OF THE GOOD SAMARITAN

H*ow did the lawyer react to Jesus' story of the good* Samaritan? Luke refrains from telling us. His omission persuades us to place ourselves on the stage and to finish the drama by journeying with Jesus down the mental road along which he leads the lawyer.

"What must I do to inherit eternal life?" "Who is my neighbor?" These questions form the starting point of the journey. "Let's start where you are," Jesus implies, "with the law. The law is good. The 'son of my house' is, most certainly, my neighbor. But the law doesn't go quite far enough. You must not only know who your neighbor is. You also need to *become* a neighbor to all—even your enemy.

"You must also recognize that there are sins of omission as well as sins of commission," Jesus continues. "Law-keepers are as capable of sinning as law-breakers. Evil cannot be categorized simply in terms of crimes a person commits. Evil also includes good that a person neglects or refuses to do.

"Then there's the misguidedness of racial hatred," Jesus insists. He makes his point powerfully by making a hated Samaritan the hero of his story. But not all is doom and gloom. Just as the glaring gap that was left by the priest and the Levite was filled by the Samaritan, so when God's trusted leaders fail him he sends other ambassadors from unexpected, even seeming enemy territory. In fact, that is precisely what God is doing in the here and now. He has rejected the religious leaders and has sent instead an outsider whom they already hate.

Just as the Samaritan in the story cared about the plight of the robbery victim, so God's new envoy cares about each individual in his world. Just as the Samaritan stooped down and poured out costly, unexpected, undeserved love on the wounded man, so God's new ambassador stoops down to God's people and lavishes undeserved love on them at great cost to himself. Just as the Samaritan brought the mugged man to safety, so God's new agent has come to mount a massive rescue operation that will secure the safety of all those who allow themselves to be rescued. Just as the Samaritan risks his life as he braves the hostility of a Jewish town, so Jesus will travel from Jericho to Jerusalem, where a cross awaits him. Just as the Samaritan compensated for the negligence of the priest and the Levite, so God's troubleshooter will more than compensate for all the omissions that have left God's people lying in pools of hurt and rejection.

Jesus and the lawyer reach the parting of the ways. The lawyer must now journey on alone. As he journeys on, doubtless he turns this story over and over in his mind. Does he recall the summary of the law: "Love God and love your neighbor"? Does his logical mind discern the implications of the order in which the two great commandments are placed? Does he realize that no one can become a neighbor to people in need in the way Jesus describes *unless* he or she is first filled with the love of God, which then overflows even to enemies? Does he see that he cannot justify himself? Does he realize that eternal life cannot be earned; it is a gift to be received? Does his clear-thinking mind suddenly discern that the rabbi with whom he has been talking face to face is, in fact, the one who is capable of offering him this gift? If so, does he scurry back to Jesus and accept the divine love so that as he continues to travel, he can offer people of every tribe and race and nation his own lesser version of this same love? Clearly this is the response that Jesus longs for him to make.

How does he respond? Both the parable and the dialogue within which it is encased are open-ended. We have no answer to the question. Instead, we must ask ourselves, "How am I responding?" One way of making this self-discovery is to meditate and pray with the cameos we have examined. That is why the rest of this chapter is devoted to some suggestions for making the story of the good Samaritan the basis for prayerful reflection.

As with the parable of the sower, there are many ways of doing this. Different people pray in different ways. Different methods of prayer help different people at different stages of their prayer pilgrimage. Therefore, if any of the suggestions I make in this section of the book seem to be hindering rather than helping your prayer, I suggest that you leave them for now. Come back to them at some future date. They might make more sense then. They might not. One of the finest pieces of prayer advice anyone has ever given is "Pray as you can, not as you can't."

Preparing to Pray

Whenever you can, before you begin to meditate on any passage of Scripture, try to prepare for your prayer in the following way:

☐ Find a place where you will be undisturbed.

☐ Find a time when you can be alone and unrushed.

☐ Transfer to God distracting troubles and excitements.

☐ Seek to become still.

☐ Open yourself to God afresh—body, mind and spirit.

☐ Ask God to give you wisdom, insight and discernment as you meditate and pray.

Having done this, one way of praying the parable is to reread Luke 10:25-37. Read it slowly and reflectively. Read it recognizing that in it Jesus highlights a series of pertinent questions:

Ethical questions: How should I live my life? How do I respond to people in need who are outside my ethnic community and/or my faith tradition?

Theological questions: How do I achieve eternal life? How am I justified before God?

Christological questions: Does the person of the good Samaritan tell me anything about the person and ministry of Jesus? If so, what?

When meditating on the parable, there is value in taking these questions in turn.

1. *Ethical questions.* Ask God to show you where you have been living your life in a way that is pleasing to him. Write down some of the things you sense you hear. Thank God for giving you the grace to live in a way that is pleasing to him. Reflect on any encounters you have had with people from other cultures or different faith traditions from yourself. How have you felt? How have you reacted? Like the priest? Like the Levite? Or like the good Samaritan?

2. *Theological questions.* Where would you place yourself on the diagram on page 98, bearing in mind that on our journey to God, we move around the circle countless times? Are you acutely aware of God's grace, God's undeserved love, at this moment? If so, are you responding to this love with heartfelt praise and acts of gratitude? Or are you resting in God and

receiving a fresh awareness of the price he paid to convince you that he loves you? Maybe, like the injured man in Jesus' story, you are lying in a pool of hurt. Maybe you are conscious of the coming of God at this painful time. Maybe, like the lawyer, you are asking basic questions: "How can I be justified before God?" If someone asked you the question the lawyer asked Jesus—"How can I be justified before God?"—what would you say?

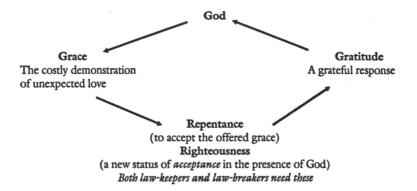

God

Grace   Gratitude
The costly demonstration   A grateful response
of unexpected love

Repentance
(to accept the offered grace)
Righteousness
(a new status of *acceptance* in the presence of God)
Both law-keepers and law-breakers need these

3. Christological questions. Go back in your imagination to your place at the back of the crowd that first hears Jesus tell the story of the good Samaritan. Listen again as Jesus tells the story. Home in on one aspect of the tale by asking yourself: "What is Jesus telling us about himself or the nature of his ministry?" Or reflect on the enormity of this claim: "The Samaritan is an unknown stranger. Yet, in spite of the cost in time, effort, money and personal danger, he freely demonstrates unexpected love to the one in need." Compare the good Samaritan with the person and ministry of Jesus.

Praying the Parable
I remember the first time I ever prayed the parable in this way. I had been rereading Ken Bailey's chapter on the good Samaritan in *Through Peasant Eyes*. I was in bed at the time, and it

happened to be Advent Sunday. I remember lying back on the pillows, stunned by the wonder of it all—that in spite of the indescribable cost to himself, Jesus entered our world, clothed himself with our humanity and poured out his life as a libation, a drink offering, for us. For me. It was as though I was hearing the good news for the first time, even though I had known it so well for decades. I lay there full of silent wonder, love and praise—longing to express God's worthiness. Eventually words began to flow. This is how I recorded my reaction in my journal:

On this Advent Sunday, Beloved, still stunned by the parable of the good Samaritan, I'm left with the question, "Who is he?" Not who is the good Samaritan. But who is this stranger who condescends to see and stop and stoop; who, out of such great compassion, hurting at gut level, compensates for all the lacks in our life? I know it's you. But who are you, Lord? Nature, resplendent in its autumn dress, gives me a clue. As I marvel at the mystery before me: the browns and bronzes of the vines, the yellowing leaves of the pomegranate trees, the silver-grays of the olives, the sapphire blue of the sea, I am reminded of who you are and how you came:

"The Creator of the sky and sea
Became a child for you and me!"[1]

That's how the Poet Laureate put it.

Yes, you created the beauty at my feet and above my head. Yet such, my Lord, was the divine condescension that you saw my plight, you saw the world's plight. You not only saw, you cared. You cared and you came. I am humbled . . . awed . . . full of heartfelt thanks.

Or I recall how I pondered this parable on my prayer walk soon after I finished writing the previous chapter. Again my mind was struggling to wrap itself around the mystery that the God who created the beauty with which I was surrounded should enter our world to demonstrate just how much he loves us. I reached my spot on the cliff where I like to pray and gazed in a stupefied kind of way at the late-afternoon sky. A bank of gray clouds occluded the setting sun. As I gazed, however, the sun suddenly burst through the cloud bank as though it were a mere grey balloon.

Gradually a coating of gold curled over the jagged edges of each piece of crumbling cloud. The splendor of the heavenly kaleidoscope filled me with awe. God, it seemed, was doing it again—bursting through the darkness with the radiance of his light, flooding the world with glory. My mind went again to Jesus, the good Samaritan's prototype, and a chorus from Handel's *Messiah* played in my mind:

Worthy is the Lamb that was slain

That has redeemed us to God by his blood

To receive power and riches and wisdom

and strength and honor and glory

and blessing

Blessing and honor, glory and power be unto him

that sitteth upon the throne

and to the Lamb.

For ever and ever

and ever and ever.

Amen.

I was glad that I was alone. My body insisted on expressing the worship that was welling up in my heart. I stood there, transfixed by the pageant of the skies and warmed by the love of the Great Samaritan himself, to whom I lifted up my arms and hands in an act of wordless adoration.

Hurting at Gut Level

As we have already noted, praying with the awareness that Jesus is the archetype of the good Samaritan does not necessarily lead us into praise. Often such prayer stems from an identification with someone else's pain—so it hurts.

When I become aware of suffering or tragedy, I sometimes find it helpful to picture the Samaritan holding the dying man in his arms or pouring oil and wine onto the man's wounds. This still-life picture of tenderness personified moves me somehow and prompts me to pray in a particular way for the spiritually and emotionally wounded.

For example, as I write, my heart keeps flying to England, where a friend of mine has just died of cancer. Ever since the news reached me, I have been placing this friend's widower into the arms of Jesus. I haven't been using many words in my prayer. Words sometimes seem to trivialize pain, I find. Instead of words, I've been picturing Jesus, the tender one, holding this widower in his arms. As time goes on, the prayer will probably change. For now, it seems enough.

I am also tuning in to the pain of a friend who has written to tell me that her marriage brings more hurt than healing. I know what the perceived rejection will be doing to this woman—pressing on pain from the past, resurrecting memories of her father's rejection. So I've been holding her too into the Great Samaritan's arms. As I've watched day after day and night after night, I've sensed him pouring healing balm into the deep wound that has been reopened in her heart so cruelly. Again, much of the prayer has been wordless but not painless. As the compassion of the Great Samaritan flows through us at such times, it can feel as though a sword pierces our own heart. That is, perhaps, hardly surprising. As we have seen, Christlike compassion means "to hurt at gut level."

Such compassion is not reserved for those we know and love. It sometimes flows from God through us to complete strangers. That has also been happening for me as I write. Before I began writing the other day, I turned on the television to watch the news. The reporter was just announcing that in Austria a bus had skidded on ice the night before. The cameras homed in on the vehicle, which had overturned and landed in the freezing waters of a lake. All but three of the passengers had been found—dead. The bodies of the deceased could be seen being dragged from their icy death beds. Horror and nausea filled me as I watched. All day I have punctuated my writing with the kind of prayer I have described—lifting the shocked relatives into the arms of the Great Samaritan—hurting at gut level as I do so.

Petitionary Prayer

Sometimes praying this particular parable gives rise not to the prayer of intercession—praying for others—but to the prayer of petition—praying for ourselves. We know that we are the ones lying stripped and naked by the roadside.

We observed in the last chapter that when the good Samaritan came on the scene, he more than compensated for the things the robbers had done and more than made up for the things the priest and the Levite refused to do. The robbers, for example, stole the man's money. The good Samaritan, on the other hand, generously payed for his accommodation at the inn. The robbers, the priest and the Levite, all abandoned him, leaving him to die in the dust. The Samaritan held him in his own arms and placed him into someone else's care. The robbers turned their backs on him. The Samaritan promised not to forsake him but to return to him.

This part of the story encourages me to believe that when we are in any kind of emotional need, it is legitimate to place ourselves in the skin of the victim of Jesus' story, to lie there in our pool of emotional blood and to wait for Jesus, the Good Samaritan, to come to minister to us. Many of us become aware, from time to time, that there have been serious lacks in our life for one reason or another. It may have been because our parents were unable or unwilling to give us the kind of loving we needed when we needed it. It may have been because of wounds inflicted by sibling rivalry or peer pressure or peer teasing. It may have been because of some kind of abuse at home, at school or elsewhere. Instead of being loved and cared for, nurtured and affirmed, accepted and cherished, we were sometimes loved, sometimes rejected, sometimes cherished, sometimes abandoned, sometimes affirmed, often criticized and so on. Although we may have repressed the pain that such ambivalence inflicted on us at the time, the grief and the loss, the sense of abandonment and rejection live on inside us, leavening the lump like yeast. It can be triggered later in life quite unexpectedly, affecting our attitudes and our behavior.

There is value at such times in simply being aware of what is happening and of lying on the Jerusalem-to-Jericho road, as it were, and letting the Great Samaritan come to us as he will. In *Listening to Others* I have written at length about such times in life and described what happened for me when I was praying this way on one occasion. A friend was praying with me at the time.

While we were waiting, silently, it was as though I "became" a baby again. . . . As I lay there alone, empty, helpless, vulnerable, I detected footsteps and later became aware of a presence. It was Jesus. He was emerging from the wood and coming to the field where I lay. When he arrived he bent over me lovingly. With one strong but tender finger I felt him stroke the downy hair on my head. That touch was comforting. He placed his finger in my tiny fist and I clutched it in the way babies delight to do. . . .

Warmth, strength, hope, even joy flooded into me as Jesus poured his fullness into my emptiness, as he met my helplessness with his sensitive strength. And as he exchanged my desolation for the consolation of his felt presence . . . I seemed to be bathed in peace.[2]

A few days later I "happened upon" a passage of Scripture that I had not consciously encountered before; it suggested to me that on that day the Great Samaritan was pouring oil and wine into pain inflicted very early on in my life.

> On the day you were born your cord was not cut, nor were you washed with water to make you clean, nor were you . . . wrapped in cloths. No one looked on you with pity or had compassion enough to do any of these things for you. Rather, you were thrown out into the open field, for on the day you were born you were despised. Then I passed by and saw you kicking about in your blood, and as you lay there in your blood I said to you, "Live!" I made you grow like a plant of the field. . . . I bathed you with water and washed the blood from you and put ointments on you. I clothed you with an embroidered dress and put leather sandals on you. I dressed you in fine linen and covered you with costly garments. I adorned you with jewelry: I put bracelets on your arms and a necklace around your neck, and I put a ring on your nose, earrings on your ears. (Ezek 16:4-12)

This beautiful, tender passage reminds us that just as the good Samaritan compensated in every way for the way others had failed to minister to the assault victim, so God can and often does make up to us for the love deprivation we lacked in the early, formative years of our life. Often this compensatory work takes place slowly and gradually, so we may find ourselves approached often and undramatically by the Great Samaritan, who continues to pour love in where there was no love, as John of the Cross expresses. His coming on such occasions is often silent, undramatic. We are not aware of what he is doing any more than the mugged man was aware of what the good Samaritan was doing. We simply become conscious that God is ministering to us in great love, continuing to tend those old wounds that can be opened up or knocked against so unexpectedly, causing us to squeal or to suffer anew.

Living Prayer

There are occasions when the roles will be reversed in our

prayer. Instead of placing ourselves in the skin of the victim, we will put ourselves in the sandals of the rescuer. A nurse who was on retreat with me did this on one occasion. She had arrived at the retreat center exhausted and in pain. She was grieving for the refugees among whom she had been working and whom she had had to leave suddenly.

"Tuck the pain into God," I suggested when she spilled out her story. "Let him minister to you." To encourage her to do this I invited her to read the story of the good Samaritan during her quiet time and to imagine that the body by the side of the road was one of the refugees she had been forced to leave behind. "Slip yourself into the good Samaritan's shoes and see what happens," I suggested.

She did. When she told me what had happened as she prayed in this way, her eyes glistened with tears. "I did what you said," she recalled. "I saw the body lying there and I went up to it. I thought it was one of the refugee women I know. I was about to dress her wounds when, suddenly, I realized that the body wasn't the woman's after all. It was Jesus. I took him in my arms and dressed his wounds. I can't explain what that did to me."

As I listened, my eyes filled with tears too, and my ears rang with a proclamation made by Jesus himself. It echoed through the corridors of my friend's mind at precisely the same moment, though neither of us spoke:

When the Son of Man comes in his glory, and all the angels with him, he will sit on his throne in heavenly glory. All the nations will be gathered before him, and he will separate the people one from another as a shepherd separates the sheep from the goats. He will put the sheep on his right and the goats on his left. Then the King will say to those on his right, "Come, you who are blessed by my Father; take your inheritance, the kingdom prepared for you since the creation of the world. For I was hungry and you gave me something to

eat, I was thirsty and you gave me something to drink, I was
a stranger and you invited me in, I needed clothes and you
clothed me, I was sick and you looked after me, I was in
prison and you came to visit me." Then the righteous will
answer him, "Lord, when did we see you hungry and feed
you, or thirsty and give you something to drink? When did
we see you a stranger and invite you in, or needing clothes
and clothe you? When did we see you sick or in prison and
go to visit you?" The King will reply, "I tell you the truth,
whatever you did for one of the least of these brothers of
mine, *you did for me.*" (Mt 25:31-40)

"You Did It for Me . . ."
Those words did for her grazed, exhausted spirit what a shot
of insulin does for a diabetic. Healing began to trickle into her
bruised heart, and it was beautiful to behold. She and I both
realized that when we're exhausted, spent and stripped because
we've expressed our gratitude to God by pouring out our lives
as a libation for others, his house is filled with fragrance. The
unique fragrance of that young nurse's life lingers on. It is with
me still.

This young woman lived her prayer. She lives it still. She
doesn't talk or write about pouring out costly, unexpected love
in the name of Christ. She does it—unobtrusively. Her praises
will never be sung in public places—only by the refugees with
whom she now works. I have a photograph of her in my study
with one of those refugees. My friend is smiling her broad,
bright smile. The refugee is smiling too as she winds her arm
around her rescuer's neck.

I could tell story after story of those who pray this parable
regularly by living it, at great cost to themselves, every day of
their lives. I think of the doctors who work in a mission hospital
in a remote part of Nepal. There I saw for myself the line of
people waiting for treatment. Many of these pathetic people,

some on crutches, some unable to stand, had walked or been carried for three or four days before they were able to join this line, which was neither orderly nor short. The doctors in this hospital treat four hundred such patients each day. They lament that they have little time to say their prayers. I, on the other hand, feel humbled when I watch them, because I become acutely aware that I am witnessing true prayer—prayer fleshed out, the prayer of the good Samaritan, the prayer that inspires me to keep on keeping on—particularly when times are tough.

Spiritual Stock-Taking

How can I live this prayer? That's one question we might ask ourselves as a result of reflecting on this parable. There are others. Richard Foster suggests that we ask ourselves questions like these each week: What opportunities for serving others has God given me this week? How did I respond? Have I encountered injustice or oppression of others during the past week? If so, was I able to work for justice and shalom? How?[3]

There are times when we may be in a situation or culture where we know that injustice exists all around us. Most of the time our hands will be tied and our lips silenced. We will be forced to form part of the conspiracy of silence that covers a multitude of sins, like the exploitation of women—particularly those from certain developing countries. Although there may be nothing we can do, there is something we can *be*. We can be a quiet, hidden, praying presence in such situations and, without realizing it, be reaping a rich harvest for God and for justice.

I think, for example, of the situation in which we find ourselves living as we do on an island that is divided—where you can be shopping in a certain street of the capital and suddenly find yourself at the so-called green line, where you are confronted with an armed guard blocking your path. I hear the pain of those who lost everything when the island fell prey to invaders: homes, possessions, loved ones, familiarity, security—

everything. There is little we can do practically, but who knows what the fruit of the prayer of the faithful will produce?

In situations like these, three questions beg to be answered:

1. What can *I* do? (Not "What can I do to inherit eternal life?" but "What can I do in this situation?")

2. Who is *my* neighbor?

3. How do I express to the people concerned that their plight hurts me at gut level? (If it does.)

Letting the Pictures Speak

One of the most powerful British TV shows I know of is *No Comment.*[4] The aim of the program is to let pictures speak for themselves, so current news is presented with a succession of film clippings, but there is no commentary, sometimes no sound at all. The pictures *do* speak for themselves. They speak eloquently and powerfully. So does the silence.

The verbal miniatures Jesus paints also speak for themselves if we will pause to ponder them in silence. They also prompt prayer. Dwell prayerfully, for example, on the picture of the thugs pouncing on, beating up, then knocking unconscious the lone traveler. Watch them snatch the man's money, then frantically tear off every stitch of his clothing. Watch them make a quick getaway, abandoning the victim to the merciless Middle Eastern sun. Let the violence you've seen on television bring the scene to life in all its vividness and horror. The story was intended to stir our emotions, not merely tickle our curiosity.

Such prayer may well become deeply disturbing. If we allow this image to play on our imagination, a flood of helplessness might threaten to overwhelm us.

I remember how this happened to me on one occasion. While praying with this particular picture, I felt prompted to watch the video *City of Joy.* Inspired by and loosely based on Dominique Lapierre's book of the same name, the film is set in Calcutta. Like the book, the film woos us into the world of the down-and-outs who inhabited the slum they called the City of Joy. There we're exposed to injustice on a massive scale: cruelty personified in the form of the mafia. There the scheming, brutality and ruthlessness of man's inhumanity to man rubs our noses in stark reality: the ugly, terrifying fact that thousands of people today live their lives like spiders caught in a gigantic, intricate and evil web of organized crime. We know this. We see evidence of it on our television screens almost every day. We watch people and nations and economies become pawns in a political game. We are aware deep down that poverty itself is organized crime. There is enough food in the world to feed all the people who inhabit planet Earth, but organized greed gives cream to the few and scarcely a crumb to the majority.

City of Joy resurrected for me the horror of some of the sights that have bruised my own spirit since I have lived overseas: the dying and destitute who eke out an existence in the slums of Delhi; the street kids of Kathmandu who are taught at a very tender age to "earn a living" from pickpocketing; the beggars who stud the pavements, subways and bridges of many major cities: Istanbul, Athens, London; the desperate little girl in Kyrgyzstan who literally clung to me as she pleaded and pleaded for money. These people tug at your heartstrings when you are with them. Then it is obvious that they are real. When we simply read about them or see their pathetic faces on the television screen, however, we can be tempted to believe that they are figments of a screenwriter's imagination. We are tempted to bury our heads in the sand. We are tempted to believe that their problem is not our problem—that it has nothing to do with us.

Perhaps, though, we need to prayerfully watch replay after replay of Jesus' picture. Perhaps we need to allow the flood waters of helplessness and hopelessness and heaviness to swirl around our hearts. Much of today's world is full of helplessness and hopelessness and heaviness. When we identify with it, the Great Intercessor, Jesus himself, can pray through us, groan

through us, weep through us, give us the privilege of copart-
nering him in his intercessory task. This horrific picture also
prepares our hearts to focus on Jesus' second miniature: the
priest passing by on the other side.

The Picture of the Priest Passing By on the Other Side
Just as praying with the picture of the traveler being attacked
might inspire us to intercede for a world that continues to hurtle
to destruction, so praying with the picture of the priest passing
by on the other side might trigger heartfelt prayer of another
kind—the kind the psalmist is famous for: the prayer that
expresses a whole medley of emotions, that leaves room for God
to speak, that moves us out of our muddled thinking into a
place of clarity and resolve.

The priest paused to weigh the facts. He wanted to deter-
mine whether it was his duty to assist the man lying in the road
or whether he could pass by with a clear conscience. He made
his decision, acted on it, and, as we saw in an earlier chapter,
was probably applauded for it. His choice, however, was pre-
dictable. He was not free to make any other.

On one occasion, while praying with this picture of the priest
pondering his options, my mood moved from anger to confession, from confession to questioning, from questioning to
release. A friend of mine had been uprooted from her country
and transplanted into a culture that left her feeling lost and
lonely, frightened and fragile. Nervously, tentatively, trustingly,
she reached out to one or two Christian people for help. They
passed her by, making it clear they were unable to come to her
aid. Like a hurting puppy, she yelped. Too far away to give her
the support she needed, I too reached out to Christian people
on her behalf. I too seemed to bump into a blank wall of
people's backs as they considered the situation and decided to
leave my friend where she was and pass her by. No one actually
used these words, but this was what they implied.

"I don't have time at the moment . . ." "I must set boundaries and make sure I keep well within them, otherwise I'll be overwhelmed . . ." "I need to prioritize . . ." "I'm not qualified to help . . ." "So-and-so might be put out if I step in . . ." "Excuses, excuses, excuses," I scribbled in my prayer journal. "Excuses, excuses, excuses," I fumed as I took my customary prayer walk.

"Whose excuses?" The question flew like a sharp arrow into my mind. I paused before confessing, "Sometimes they're my excuses." The realization hit me like a bolt of lightning. Others, I realized, were meting out the learned responses that I myself sometimes give. *These reasons are merely variations on a theme,* I thought, *the priest's objections dressed up in twentieth-century Western jargon. They result in my making my choice and often being applauded for making it.* I felt chastened, contrite, calm—repentant in the sense that I longed to learn to live differently.

"But how do I live differently, Lord?" I questioned. "There's a vast ocean of need out there. If its waves pound the beach of my life, I don't know what will become of me. I'll be swamped. Swallowed up. Devoured." I paused. A few moments later, I sensed I saw God smiling in amusement. "I know you're not Hercules," he seemed to say. "Don't misunderstand this parable. I'm not asking you to carry the whole world on your shoulders. I'm not a hard taskmaster. My yoke is easy."

My mind went back to the film *City of Joy.* One of the main characters in the film is an American doctor, Max. "I hate being a doctor!" he exploded when someone begged him to become the slum's physician. He made it clear that he had no intention of staying in Calcutta to be a good Samaritan to the city's sick and dying. He despised such "do-goodery." Angry young man that he was, such service as he gave to the people around him was dutiful rather than willing. Gradually, though, his heart softened. Love was melting it—the love the lepers poured into him and the genuine admiration and affection that individual refugees showered on him. Eventually the constant drip of the genuineness of true friendship eroded his hardness.

"I'm glad to be here," he confessed to his colleague one day. "I feel so alive. I'm glad I came." Knowing of the struggles he had worked through and knowing that he had been offered a job in America, she replied: "Now you're free to go." With a look of peace lighting up his face, he insisted, "Now I'm free to stay." He was free to stay because he wanted to stay. He was free to stay because the hurt inside him that had been inflicted by his father when he was a child had been healed by the love his despised, disreputable patients were pouring into him.

I thought again of the confession I had made, the remorse that I had felt and the fear that I can't become the neighbor God wants me to become lest I should be swamped by people's needs. I thought again of Jesus' insistence that he is not laying on us a heavy burden.

Over a period of days I continued to pray with this part of the parable. As I did so, I was reminded of the rich young ruler who came to Jesus and asked him the same question as the lawyer asked: "Good teacher, what must I do to inherit eternal life?" (Lk 18:18). Jesus answered his question with undeniable clarity: "You still lack one thing. Sell everything you have and give to the poor" (v. 22). *These were specific instructions given to a particular person who asked an incisive question at a precise moment,* I reasoned. Jesus might or might not ask me to sell everything and give the money to the poor. My mind went again to the lawyer who was handicapped by the very law that was supposed to bring him closer to God. "What must I do to inherit eternal life?" he had asked. According to Jesus, what he needed to do was to break free from a religious system that was keeping him from receiving the God-life he craved. Jesus wanted to give the lawyer the internal freedom to draw alongside the needy whether they fall into the Pharisees' narrow definition of the word *neighbor* or not.

"Lord, show me what I need," I begged.

"You too need to be set free," came the reply. "You need to be set free from the compulsion of your own compassion. I'm not asking you to become a neighbor to the whole world. I am asking you to keep your eyes on me as a lover watches the beloved. The look in my eye will prompt you when and where and how to respond to my call to care. The compassion I give you will equip you to go, to care, to cope. It is my love that heals, not yours. It is my love that consoles, not yours. It is my love that rescues, not yours."

The prayer that had begun on a crescendo of anger and moved through many emotions ended on a diminuendo of understanding, relinquishment and peace. Although quiet—even hushed—it was a wonderfully liberating moment. A weight seemed to have been lifted off my heart as I noted again that love received and given is the key to this memorable story.

I didn't consciously continue to pray with this part of the parable in the weeks that followed. I found, however, that the parable was, as it were, being prayed within me. Much of my "spiritual reading" seemed to underline the emphasis that had come to me while I was meditating on the story. Jesus' own definition of the phrase "eternal life," for example, seemed to leap from the page of the book I was reading right into the lap of my heart: "Now this is eternal life: [to] know you, the only true God, and Jesus Christ, whom you have sent" (Jn 17:3). "Eternal life is 'to know God.' "[5]

The number-one priority is to know him and become intimate with him. The closer I come to him, the more I will catch his compassion and the more I will discern where and when and how he wants me to act and react in any given situation. But I must always balance "the compulsion of compassion" with his example. As Sister Margaret Magdalene expresses:

He refused to submit to the tyranny of the urgent. He would not let the crowds or even human need dictate the priorities

He had the inner freedom to say "No." . . . Not in bondage
to the need to achieve, nor neurotic about the success of his
mission, nor puffed up by popularity, he is free. He can weave
his way safely through the continual manipulation of men.
Simply because he has been alone, he is in touch with the
wellsprings of his life. . . . It is not easy to stand by in an
apparent impotence, but we have to turn away resolutely
from any Messiah-complex which tries to do everything and
in the end achieves very little.[6]

Praying the parable underscored for me again that the main
thrust of Jesus' story is not "Go and bandage the wounds of
everyone everywhere." Rather, through the parable, Jesus is
pleading with us, implying, "Receive the divine love so that
when the call comes, you are ready to respond and let his love
flow through you."

Personalizing the Prayer
One of the most powerful ways of praying this particular
parable, I find, is to personalize it. One way of doing this is to
take a trip down memory lane, asking questions like these:

☐ When have I needed a neighbor in Jesus' sense of the word?
Who came to me on those occasions? What happened? How
did it feel?

☐ When did I lie abandoned on the edge of life's journey? Did
anyone take a peep at me and then pass me by? How did that
feel?

☐ When have I been physically, emotionally or spiritually raped
or mugged? How did it feel? Does the memory draw me to
people in similar need? Or does it repel me?

Each of these questions could draw you deeper and deeper
into Jesus' story. Each of the questions could trigger a prayer
of the heart. Let it flow from you onto paper, knowing that the
eyes of the great Storyteller will read it. Then venture out into
your corner of the world and watch it being transformed by

today's "good Samaritans." I watched one while I was writing this chapter. He's old. Probably illiterate. He was sitting on a hard wooden chair outside his humble home spoon-feeding an emaciated, gray-haired skeleton of a woman I took to be his wife. The picture was so packed with the beauty of tenderness personified that I stood in the shadows and took a mental photograph. I'd like it to be engraved on my mind forever. Such scenes inspire me and goad me into living as well as praying this unforgettable story of the good Samaritan.

THE MOST
MEMORABLE
PARABLE
OF THEM ALL

J*ust before they left Cyprus, Ken Bailey and his wife visited the* part of the island where we live. Soon after daybreak one sun-splashed Sunday, we drove into the hills. On a secluded picnic site affording a breathtaking view of the shimmering sea and the sweep of coast known as the Bay of Gold, Ken lit a wood and charcoal fire on which we cooked breakfast. "Just like Jesus barbecued fish on the beach for his disciples," we recalled. We didn't barbecue fish but scrambled eggs, sizzled bacon and toasted bread. Sitting around that cheerful fire, warmed by the rays of the rising sun, we savored the taste of the bacon and the smell of the singed toast. We also reminisced, attempted to peep into the future and lamented the pain of saying goodby.

During a lull in the conversation, my husband drew from his

rucksack a portable Communion set. The chatter ceased. Apart from the chorus chanted by the birds, a hush fell on us. We prepared ourselves to pray the most mysterious parable Jesus ever told.

In Hebrew and Arabic, as we saw in chapter one, the word *parable* embraces a whole variety of figurative speech—including symbols. On the night he was betrayed, sharing that meal with his disciples we now call the Last Supper, Jesus took bread from the table, held it high for all to see, turned his eyes heavenward, blessed the bread and then uttered that immortal parable: "This is my body, given for you . . ." After supper, he did something similar with the goblet of wine, giving the disciples another unforgettable parable: "This is my blood, poured out for you . . ."

As I prepared the soil of my heart to receive this uniquely precious seed, I tried to step into the upper room so that I could be present at the Last Supper. I placed myself behind the disciples so that I could receive Jesus' mystery through their eyes, their ears, their perception. As Jesus spoke, however, I sensed that the disciples were as dumbfounded as I still am by those pregnant words. I couldn't begin to fathom how the disciples might be receiving them. Instead, as the service progressed, I seemed to see Jesus coming toward me, standing in front of me, saying to me: "Take, eat . . . drink . . ." Moved and humbled, I did as he invited. I received the bread and the wine from his own hands. As I ate, as I drank, as I savored and as I relished these sacred symbols, I recognized that they were fusing with me and I with them. They were nourishing me and giving me strength.

I marveled afresh at the humility of the divine Lover who takes a piece of bread in his hands, holds it out and pleads: "Take, eat . . ." We might well refuse. He therefore runs the risk of rejection.

My mind went, inevitably, to this book, which I was to begin writing the next day. I wanted to write that the purpose of Jesus' parables is to press his hearers to make a response. I prayed then, as I pray now, that those who embark on the adventure of praying the parables may find themselves irresistibly drawn by the Storyteller himself to make that heart-response that he longs for us to make. That response unlocks the gateway to freedom, fruitfulness and unending fellowship with him.

Notes

Introduction
[1]Ruth Burrows, *To Believe in Jesus* (London: Sheed and Ward, 1981), p. 79.
[2]Kenneth E. Bailey, *Poet and Peasant and Through Peasant Eyes* (Grand Rapids, Mich.: Eerdmans, 1983).
[3]T. W. Manson's phrase.

Chapter 1: The Purpose & Power of the Parable
[1]Alfred Edersheim, *The Life and Times of Jesus the Messiah* (Grand Rapids, Mich.: Eerdmans, 1901), p. 581.
[2]Eugene Peterson's paraphrase of Matthew 5:21ff., *The Message* (Colorado Springs, Colo.: NavPress, 1994).
[3]Matthew 13:13 *The Message*.
[4]Matthew 13:11-14 *The Message*. My emphasis.
[5]Kenneth E. Bailey, *Finding the Lost* (St. Louis, Mo.: Concordia, 1992), p. 18.
[6]S. McFague Te Selle, *Speaking in Parables*, quoted in ibid.
[7]T. W. Manson, *The Teaching of Jesus* (Cambridge: Cambridge University Press, 1935), quoted by Bailey in *Poet and Peasant*, p. 39.

Chapter 2: Keys That Unlock the Parables
[1]Bailey, *Poet and Peasant*, p. 35.
[2]Ibid., pp. 161-62.
[3]Ibid., p. 35.
[4]Ibid., p. 41.

Chapter 3: Understanding the Parable of the Sower
[1]This phrase was coined earlier in the twentieth century by Cambridge scholar John Oman. It is a phrase that captured the imagination of Ken Bailey and that he and I once discussed.
[2]W. H. Vanstone's phrase.
[3]Sue Monk Kidd's phrase in *When the Heart Waits* (San Francisco: Harper & Row, 1990).

Chapter 4: Praying the Parable of the Sower
[1]Lyrics, Brian Doerksen. Music © Mercy Publishing/Kingsway's Thankyou Music.
[2]*The Message.*
[3]E.g., *Open to God, Listening to God, The Smile of Love* (London: Hodder & Stoughton).
[4]Kidd, *When the Heart Waits,* p. 22.
[5]Maria Boulding, *Gateway to Hope* (London: Fount Paperbacks, 1985), p. 41.

Chapter 5: Understanding the Parable of the Good Samaritan
[1]Bailey, *Poet and Peasant,* p. 37.
[2]Ibid., p. 43.
[3]Ben Sirach. Quoted in ibid., pp. 43-44, Ken Bailey's emphasis.
[4]I have been drawing heavily here on the insights of Ken Bailey as spelled out in *Poet and Peasant.*
[5]Bailey, *Poet and Peasant,* p. 47.
[6]My adaptation of the questions Richard Foster has his Renovare groups asking themselves, from *Renovare: Where New Life Begins* (booklet), available from Renovare, P.O. Box 879, Wichita, KS 67201-0879.
[7]Rene Philombwo, a Cameroon writer quoted by J. Veltri in *Orientations* (Chicago: Loyola University Press, 1979), p. 7.

Chapter 6: The Good Samaritan
[1]Bailey, *Poet and Peasant,* p. 54.
[2]Matthew 14:14; 20:34; 1:14; 15:32; 9:36; Mark 8:2; Luke 7:13.

Chapter 7: Praying the Parable of the Good Samaritan
[1]John Betjeman.
[2]Joyce Huggett, *Listening to Others* (London: Hodder & Stoughton, 1988), pp. 185, 186.
[3]My adaptation of questions that appear in Richard Foster's *Renovare: Where New Life Begins.*
[4]*No Comment.* Transmitted on Euronews.
[5]Thomas A. Green, *When the Well Runs Dry* (Notre Dame, Ind.: Ave Maria Press, 1992), p. 66.
[6]Sister Margaret Magdalene, *Jesus, Man of Prayer* (London: Hodder & Stoughton, 1987), pp. 41, 42, 52.